Mel Bay's

DELUXE JAZZ & ROCK BASS METHOD

by Vincent Bredice

A stereo cassette tape of the music in this book is now available. The publisher strongly recommends the use of this cassette tape along with the text to insure accuracy of interpretation and ease in learning.

Foreword

The material in this method, when absorbed, will teach a student the essentials of the jazz and rock idioms. The author has endeavored to present an approach which will guarantee a musical foundation and an expertise in technique and theory that is applicable to the needs of all bass players. Reading and rhythms are stressed throughout the book. The material deals in great depth with the construction and function of all scales, modes and harmonies along with many patterns and ideas using the major, minor, 2 diminished, augmented, major pentatonic, minor pentatonic and blues scales.

The modes treated are the ionian, dorian, phrygian, lydian, lydian dominant, lydian augmented, lydian augmented dominant, aeolian, locrian, locrian #2, locrian ♭4, along with the harmonies that they play through.

Ear training, transposition, modulation, syncopation, duets, progressions, substitutions, chord movements, blues progressions are discussed with examples and are made palatable for the players in all positions throughout the bass. There are 2 octave fingerings of the above scales, modes and harmonies.

The author uses the five steps in learning. These are:

(1) Theory — (2) Singing & hearing (3) Playing the material in the entire spectrum of the instrument. (4) Inventing patterns (5) Development of ideas.

Finally, it is very difficult to master this material the first time through the book and the student is advised to use his best friend and ally—**Review**, one of the finest teachers in music.

Vincent Bredice

Table of Contents

The Essential Fundamentals of Music

5 Lines   4 Spaces

Each line and space is lettered using the first seven letters of the alphabet.

Five lines   Four spaces

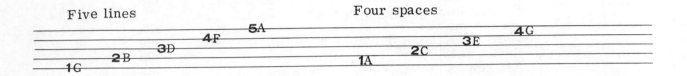

The Bass Clef 𝄢 is used to notate music for the bass guitar.

Bass or F clef

Notice that the two dots are above and below the 4th line (F line). This is why we call it the F clef.

The staff is divided into measures by vertical lines called bar lines.

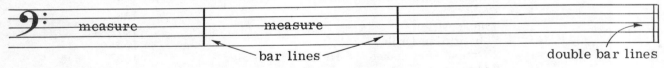

measure   measure

bar lines   double bar lines

Note Values

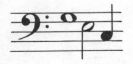

A whole note receives four counts or four beats.
A half note receives two counts or two beats.
A quarter note receives one count or one beat.

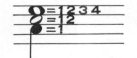

Time Signature

4/4 or (C) are called time signatures. We call this common time.

4 - 4 Counts to a measure
4 - A Quarter note = one beat

3/4 = 3 Counts to a measure   2/4 = 2 Counts to a measure
      Quarter note = 1 beat   Quarter note = 1 beat
   ¢   = Alla breve called cut time   = 1 beat (2 counts per measure)

Rests

Every note has a corresponding rest. A rest means not to play for a certain number of beats.

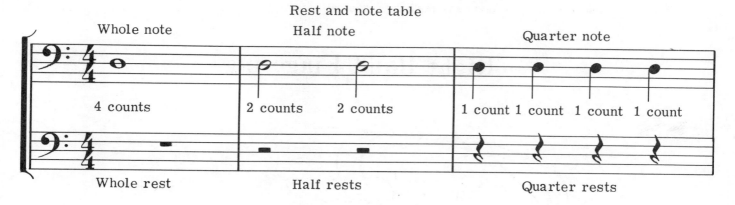

Rest and note table

The Dot

A dot placed after a note increases the value of that note by 1/2 of its value.

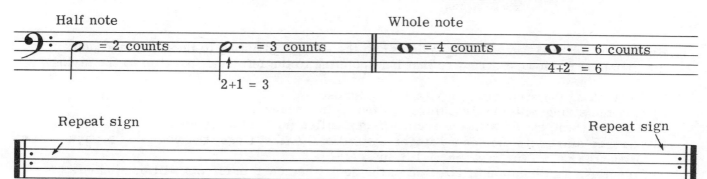

The two dots placed at the beginning and end of a piece mean to repeat the piece.

The sign ⨟ means to repeat what immediately preceded it.

1) Repeat previous measure   2) Repeat previous two beats

Test on Fundamentals of Music

In the following test the student is to find the following:

F clef
Staff
Five lines   A whole note and a whole rest   Time signature
Four spaces   Half note and a half rest   Dotted half note
Bar lines   Quarter note and a quarter rest   Repeat signs
measures

Continue with this test and name the **lines + spaces**

Right Hand Fingering

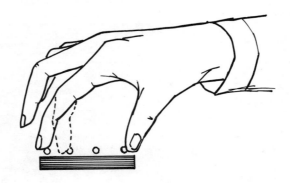

Hold the right hand fingers perpendicular to the strings (pointing to the floor) and place the thumb on the lowest string so that it is pointing to the left hand (parallel to the string)

When stroking the string use an alternating stroke.
1) Play the string with the first finger called (i) index finger.
2) Play the same string with the second finger called (m) middle finger.
3) You may start with the second finger instead of the first finger but you must always alternate the two fingers. (m, i,) (i, m,) etc.
4) Do not use the thumb until later on in the book when certain effects will be studied.
5) Never stroke from the inside of the string pulling it away from the base. The correct stroking is to stroke the string (as though you were fondling a child or a pet) and continue the finger action until you rest against the next string.
6) Always play with volume in your early stages of learning. Although this will prove a little difficult at first, you eventually will develop speed, control, and a good sound.
7) Repeated fingering can be used in very slow tempos.
8) A major point to be concerned with is that you alternate fingers when you change strings. If you play a note on the G first string with the m finger and the next note is on the D second string, be sure to use the i finger. Using the m finger for both strings constitutes gliding – a very poor habit to cultivate as it denies the performer control and speed.

8

The four open strings
There are four strings on the bass guitar: G first string, D second string, A third string,
(E fourth string.)
(Lowest in pitch)

Tuning the Bass

The bass player should purchase a pitch pipe and practice matching the strings to the given sounds on the pipe.

How to tune the bass without the aid of the pitch pipe.

1) Stroke the open G string. Place your finger on the 5th fret of the second D string and while pressing this 5th fret, turn the D string tuning peg until the sound of the D string equals the open G string.
2) Stroke the tuned D string and pressing on the 5th fret of the 3rd or A string, Turn the A string tuning peg until the A string sound matches the open D string Sound.
3) Play the tuned A string and pressing the 5th fret of the E fourth string turn the E string tuning peg until the E string sounds the same as the A string sound. This puts you in tune with yourself. When you play with other musicians, you must all tune to one given pitch and then you tune accordingly.

Tuning with the Keyboard Instruments

You can tune with the piano and organ as following:

Piano or organ keyboard

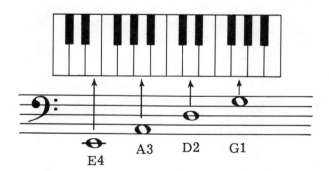

E4   A3   D2   G1

1) Strike E on the piano and then turn your E string tuning peg until you are in "tune".
2) Do this with the other 3 strings.

Bass guitar notation

The Notated Four Open Strings

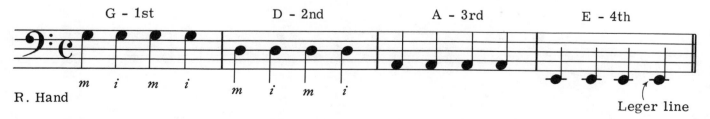

G - 1st   D - 2nd   A - 3rd   E - 4th

R. Hand

Leger line

The line placed through, above or below a note not on the staff is called a leger line.

9

Exercise for Alteration of Right Hand Stroking

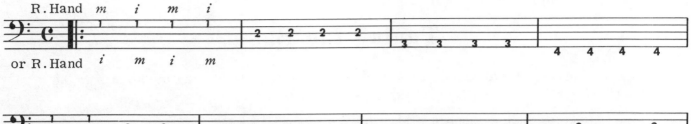

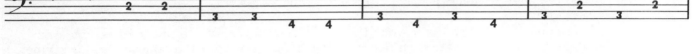

Repeat sign

Open String Exercise

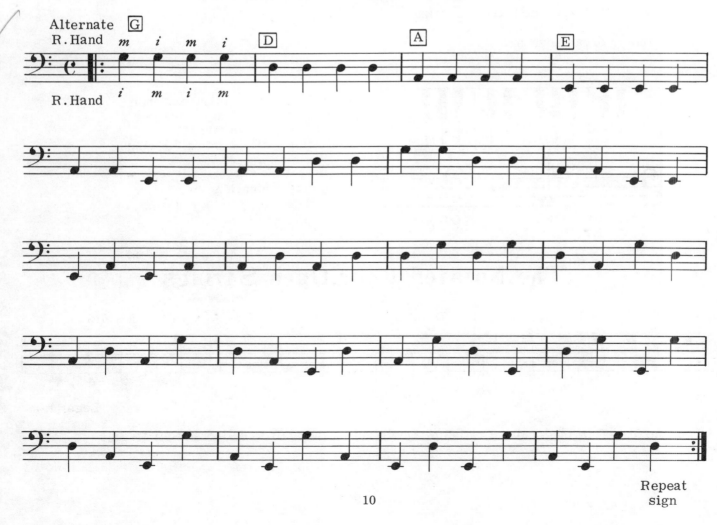

Repeat sign

The Left Hand

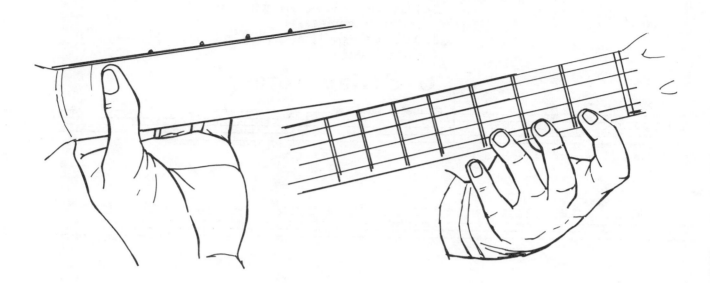

Place your thumb behind the neck opposite the first or second fret in a vertical position. The thumb should not protrude above the top of the bass neck so that it can be seen from the front side of the bass. This is important as holding the thumb correctly allows the wrist to be sufficiently arched so that the fingers can be curved and press the strings with fingertip control.

Press the string next to the fret bar closest to the next higher fret and press with substantial force.

Correct position of the hands and volume are the two results that you are looking for. Speed will come gradually as the correct muscles are developed. Never allow the palms of either hand to touch the instrument.

The Notes on the First String [G]

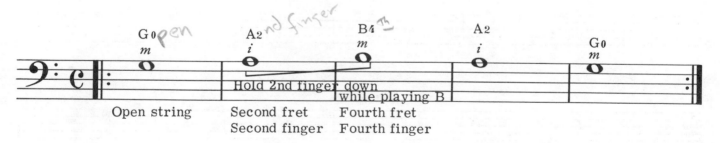

Exercise on the G String

How to practice: 1) Always name notes before playing.
2) Play with volume and with correct thumb placement.
3) Alternate: (m i, m i) or (i m, i m.)
4) Count aloud

G String Notes

Count 1 2 3 4

Rhythm on the G String

A definition of rhythm is counting. (Thumb?)

Count 1 2 3 4 1 2 3 4 1 2 3 4

Take
finger off
on 4th beat

The Notes on the D 2nd String

When F is followed by E, hold your second finger down while pressing with your third finger. This teaches: 1) finger independence (any finger is able to move while another is stationary) 2) finger strengthening (for the same reason) 3) fret distances (the finger learns to stretch correct distances)

Exercise on the D String

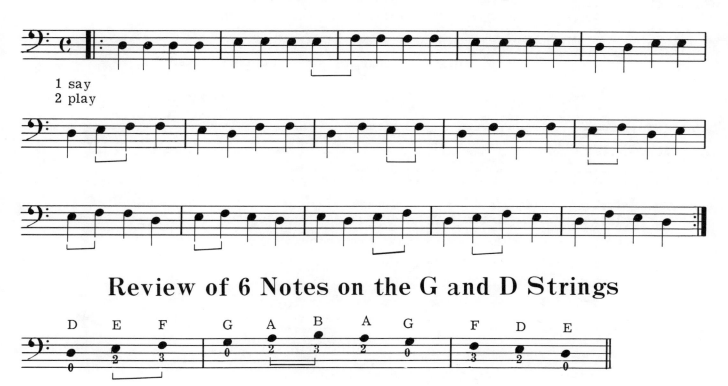

1 say
2 play

Review of 6 Notes on the G and D Strings

Exercise on the G and D Strings

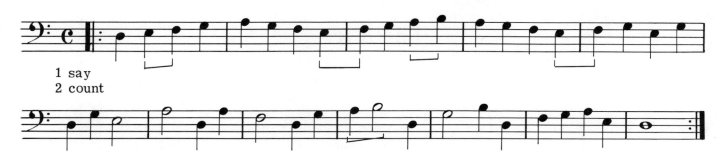

1 say
2 count

13

Chromatic or Accidental Signs

A sharp (♯) raises the pitch of a note one fret. (Press the next fret to the right.)

A flat (♭) lowers the pitch of a note one fret. (Press the next fret to the left.)

A natural (♮) cancels the sharp or flat.

The Chromatic Notes on the G String

Open string	1st fret	3rd fret	3rd fret	1st fret	4th fret
	1st finger	3rd finger	3rd finger	1st finger	4th finger

The word enharmonic means - Same sound different spelling   ex. G♯ = A♭
Both are played on the same fret.

The Chromatic Notes on the D String

Open string	1st fret	3rd fret	4th fret	2nd fret	1st fret
	1st finger	3rd finger	4th finger	2nd finger	1st finger

The student must commit these sharp and flat notes to memory.

The Natural

Cancels the A♭ sign

Still G♯ until the next measure

Cancels the D♯

Bar line cancels the D♯

Cancels the F sharp

The Tie

The tie is a curved line that connects two notes of the same pitch. The first note is played but the second note is not played but is counted as part of the first note time value.

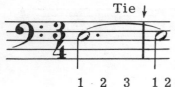

Tie ↓

1 · 2 · 3   1 2 = 5 counts

Example: Play the 1st E dotted half note, count 3 beats, hold it over the bar line, count 2 more beats but do not play the second note E.

14

Notes on the A 3rd String

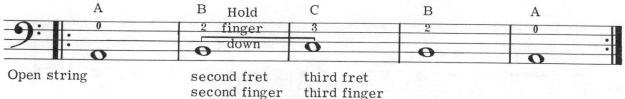

Exercise on the A Third String

Chromatic Notes on the A String

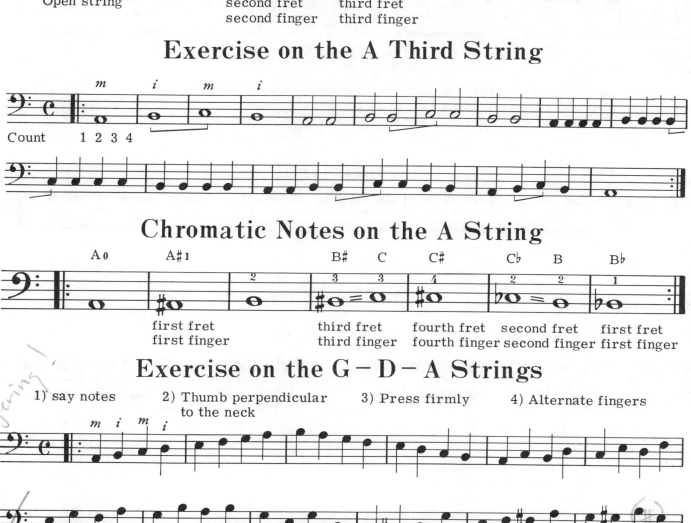

Exercise on the G – D – A Strings

1) say notes   2) Thumb perpendicular to the neck   3) Press firmly   4) Alternate fingers

4th fret

A string

Eighth Notes

There are two eighth notes in one quarter note, we count eighth notes using the symbols "1" "+"

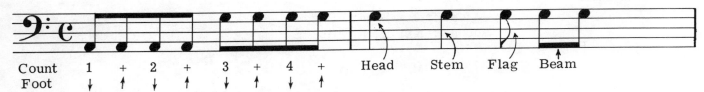

Count	1	+	2	+	3	+	4	+

Head   Stem   Flag   Beam

Eighth rest - ♪ = An eighth rest and it has the same value as an eighth note.
In common time we give 1/2 of a beat to an 1/8 note.
Two 1/8 notes = 1 beat. Always use the word "and " when counting.
We divide the beat in two parts. - down up (the "up" is the "and")

1/8 Note Drill

Alternate   *m   i   m   i*

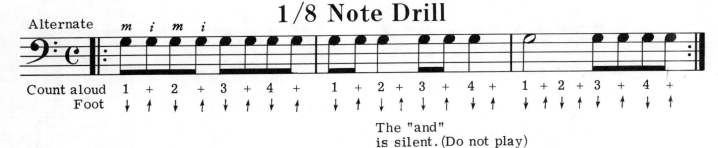

Count aloud   1 + 2 + 3 + 4 +   1 + 2 + 3 + 4 +   1 + 2 + 3 + 4 +
Foot

The "and"
is silent. (Do not play)

This must be memorized.

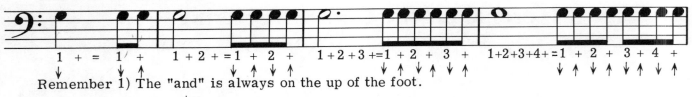

1 + = 1 +   1 + 2 + = 1 + 2 +   1+2+3+=1 + 2 + 3 +   1+2+3+4+=1 + 2 + 3 + 4 +

Remember 1) The "and" is always on the up of the foot.
2) The number is always on the down of the foot.
3) Always count aloud.
4) Always alternate
5) We need two 1/8 notes to make a complete beat.

Combinations of 1/8 Note Drills

m   i m i m   i m i m i

1 + 2 + 3 + 4 +   1 + 2 + 3 + 4 +   1 + 2 + 3 + 4 +   1 + 2 + 3 + 4 +   1+2+3+ 4 +

1/8 Note Rest Drills

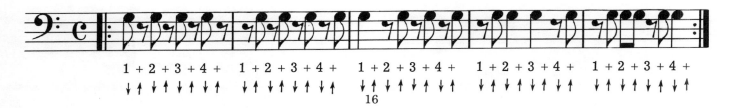

1 + 2 + 3 + 4 +   1 + 2 + 3 + 4 +   1 + 2 + 3 + 4 +   1 + 2 + 3 + 4 +   1 + 2 + 3 + 4 +

Slowly then fast. Exercise on the G - D - A strings using 1/8 notes.

Alternate

Continue

Count

The E 4th String

E	F	F#	G	G#	Ab
0	1	2	3	4	4

| Open string | First fret
First finger | Second fret
Second finger | Third fret
Third finger | Fourth fret
Fourth finger | Fourth fret
Fourth finger |

Gb	Fb	Open	First fret	Second fret	Fourth fret

Second fret
Second finger

Open

E = Fb   E# = F   F# = Gb   G# = Ab

The E String Drill

Remember the bar line
cancels the flat

Gb   G♮

(F♮)

17

The Chromatic Scale

The word chrome means to color. In the chromatic scale, we color all notes, that is to say we play a note on each fret ascending using sharps and descending using flats.
The chromatic scale is the octave divided into twelve equal notes.

Chromatic Scale on 4 Strings

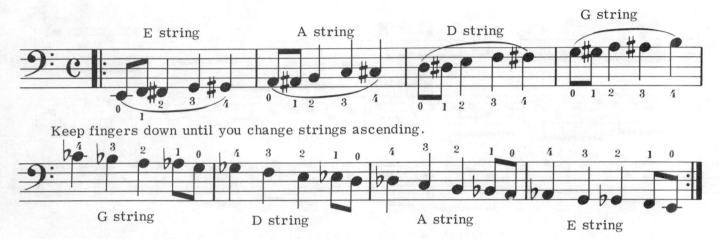

Keep fingers down until you change strings ascending.

This is an excellent technique builder and should be practiced daily.
1) Always play with top volume.
2) Press your left fingers firmly.
3) Keeping the right hand relaxed, use rest stroke alternating finger technique with maximum volume at first and later play lightly trying for speed but even movement.

Chromatic Drill

Always keep fingers down until you change strings.

The Dotted Quarter Note

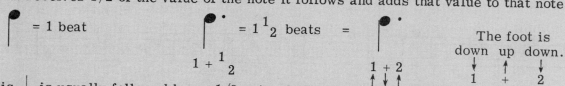

A dot receives 1/2 of the value of the note it follows and adds that value to that note.

♩ = 1 beat   ♩. = 1 1/2 beats = ♩.

1 + 1/2   1 + 2   The foot is
                                              down up down.
                                              1   +   2

This ♩. is usually followed by an 1/8 note which will receive 1/2 of a beat and completes the two beats.

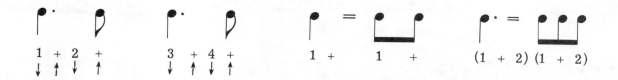

1 + 2 +   3 + 4 +   1 +   1 +   (1 + 2) (1 + 2)

Alternate

Count   1 + 2 + 3 + 4 +   1 + 2 + 3 + 4 +
Foot

Dotted Quarter Note and 1/8 Note Drill

1 + 2 + 3 + 4 +

Drill Number Two

1 + 2 + 3 + 4 +   1 + 2 + 3 + 4 +

A Review of the G – D – A – E Strings & Rhythms

Chromatic Octave Drill

The 5th - 6th - 7th - 8th frets on the G string
These new notes are needed to construct the C -(C# / D♭) - D - E♭ Major scales.

The Major Scale

To construct a major scale think of a series of 8 notes in alphabetical order with a half step between the third and fourth and seventh and eighth notes. All other notes are separated by a whole step. (1/2 step = 1 fret - A whole step = 2 frets).

The G Major Scale

1) Write the letters.
   1 2 3 4 5 6 7 8
   G A B C D E F G

2) Write a note above each letter.

3) Mark the 1/2 steps. Notice that the 7th and 8th notes are one step apart but should be 1/2 step apart. Also notice that the 6th and 7th notes are 1/2 step apart but should be 1 step apart.

By inserting a sharp before the note F we now have the 1/2 step needed between the 7th and 8th notes F and G and also the whole step needed between the 6th and 7th notes E and F. All major scales will have the following pattern regardless of the note you start with.

MAJOR SCALE PATTERN
1) Write any note
2) Next note is 2 frets away
3) Next note is 2 frets away
4) Next note is 1 fret away
5) Next note is 2 frets away
6) Next note is 2 frets away
7) Next note is 2 frets away
8) Next note is 1 fret away

The correct G major scale.

G major has 1 sharp (F#)
The 1/2 steps lie between
the (3/4) + (7/8) notes.

Construct the F Major Scale

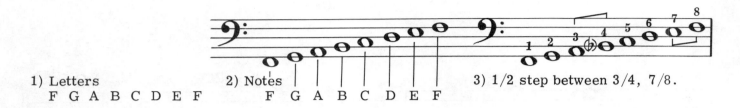

1) Letters   2) Notes   3) 1/2 step between 3/4, 7/8.

F G A B C D E F   F G A B C D E F

Notice that between the notes A and B there is 1 step. As A and B are the 3rd and 4th notes and should be separated by 1/2 step, we lower the B to B♭. We now have the corrected F major scale.

Scale of F major has 1 flat (B♭)

How to const-
ruct the A♭ scale

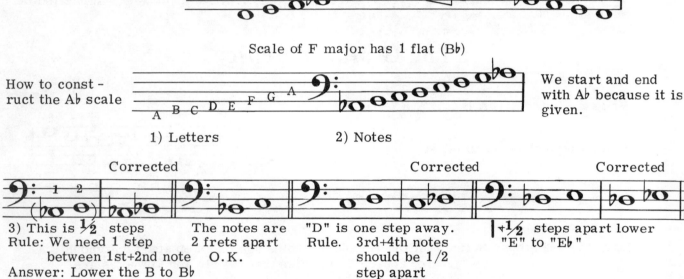

A B C D E F G A

We start and end with A♭ because it is given.

1) Letters   2) Notes

| Corrected | Corrected | Corrected |

3) This is ½ steps
Rule: We need 1 step
    between 1st+2nd note
Answer: Lower the B to B♭

The notes are
2 frets apart
O.K.

"D" is one step away.
Rule. 3rd+4th notes
should be 1/2
step apart
lower "D" to
"D♭"

+1½ steps apart lower
"E" to "E♭"

A♭ scale

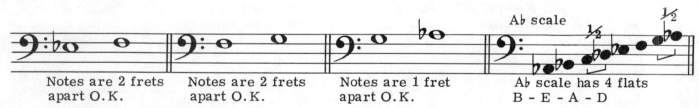

Notes are 2 frets
apart O.K.

Notes are 2 frets
apart O.K.

Notes are 1 fret
apart O.K.

A♭ scale has 4 flats
B - E - A - D

The student should now practice constructing the major scales on the following notes and play them ascending and descending.

Formula 1

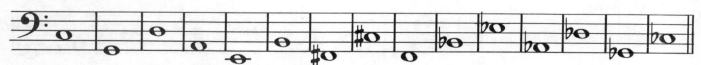

Notice the C major scale has no sharps and no flats when we write the alphabetical formula. The half steps and whole steps are correct without any addition of sharps or flats.

1) Play whole range of bass (down to lowest note)
2) Keep it all in 1st fret position (except high notes, of course)
3) Don't substitute fingers. 1st fret = 1st finger etc.

After the scales have been written, the student can check with the scales below for corrections.

Play all scales at all times using *m i* or *i m*, correct hand position, and with volume.

The 15 Major Scales

The sooner these scales are memorized, the more rapid the progress.

How to Practice Scales

This is the beginning of daily technical exercises that the student should cultivate. Start your habits correctly and you will be amazed how much you will improve. Think of a plant growing without weeds.

Invent your own patterns. Learning and hearing scale patterns is one facet of music that must be learned somewhere in any complete approach to an instrument.

Sixteenth Notes

There are 4/16 notes to a quarter note. 4/16 = 1/4
There are 2/16 notes to an eighth note. 2/16 = 1/8
We use the symbols 1a+a to count sixteenth notes.

Count   1 a + a 2 a + a 3 a + a 4 a + a
Foot

1 e + a 2 e + a

Steps to learn to count sixteenth notes: 1) play with no counting

Notice that there are 2 sixteenth notes on the down of the foot and 2 sixteenth notes on the up of the foot. (up is always the "and")

Alternate ①

② 2) Play and count aloud.

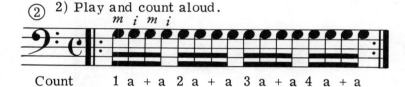

Count   1 a + a 2 a + a 3 a + a 4 a + a

Keep notes evenly

3) Play 2 notes on the down of the foot
And 2 notes on the up of the foot.
no counting.

③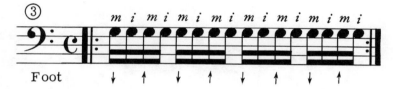

Foot

4) Play and count and use your foot.

④

Count aloud 1 a + a   2 a + a   3 a + a   4 a + a
Foot

Sixteenth note drill using the G major scale.

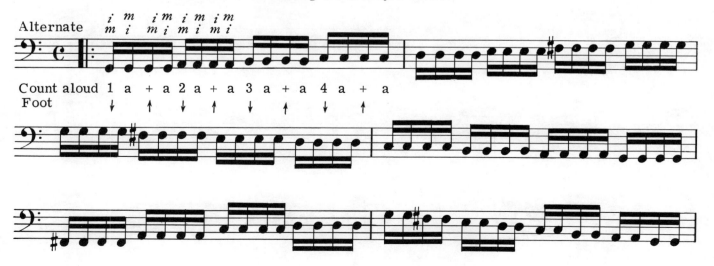

Count aloud 1 a   + a 2 a + a 3 a + a 4 a   +   a
Foot

The Major Scales Using 1/16 Note Figures

The Major Scale and the Modes That It Generates

From the major scale, we can form other <u>scales called modes.</u> The major scale is called the ionian mode. On each note of the major scale, we can form the following 6 modes:
1) From the note D to the note D one octave higher = The dorian mode
2) From the note E to the note E one octave higher = The phrygian mode
3) From the note F to the note F one octave higher = The lydian mode
4) From the note G to the note G one octave higher = The mixolydian mode
5) From the note A to the note A one octave higher = The aeolian mode
6) From the note B to the note B one octave higher = The locrian mode
These modes must be played ascending and descending and memorized.

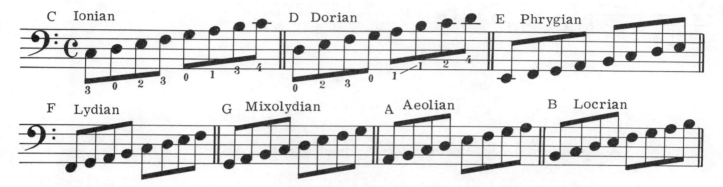

Major Scale Patterns on the 4 Strings

When we play a scale without open strings, it can be played in any position on the bass by moving all notes and fingers up or down the fingerboard retaining the same finger pattern that we start with.

This is a pattern scale starting on the root.

G♭ major scale   Root= name of scale

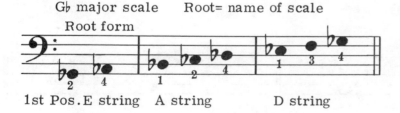

1st Pos. E string   A string   D string

There are no open strings therefore it is a moveable scale. By moving the notes up one fret, we move up to the second position and play the G major scale. Move everything up one more fret and we play the A♭ 3rd position scale.

A position is determined by the placement of the 1st finger. In the 1st position, the 1st finger is on the 1st fret, the 2nd finger is on the 2nd fret, the 3rd finger is on the 3rd fret, and the 4th finger is on the 4th fret.

G Major Scale - Root form (same finger pattern as the G♭ major scale above.)

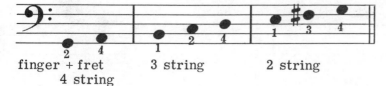

finger + fret   3 string   2 string
   4 string

Move this G major pattern up one fret and we play the A♭ major scale.

This is a pattern scale starting on the 3rd note of the scale. (Phrygian mode sound)

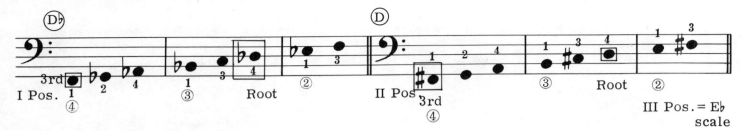

Pattern scale starting on the 5th (Mixolydian sound)

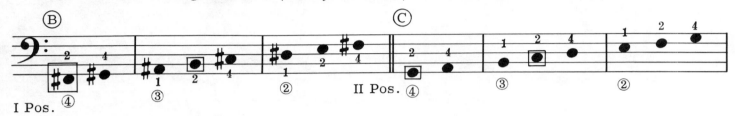

The Fret Guide

The fret guide is invaluable for pattern ideas. Memorize it.

It simply means that these letter notes will be found next to each other anywhere on the guitar. Example: The note B♭ will always follow the note A; The note E♭ will always follow the note D on any string or position.

When one pattern idea is learned, you have learned twelve pattern ideas.

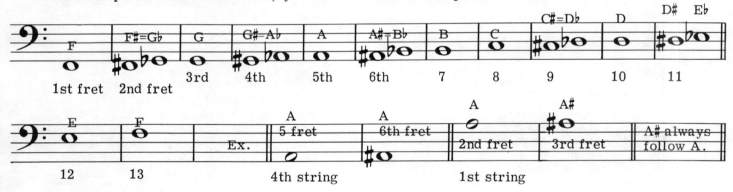

Major Pattern Scales on the A String

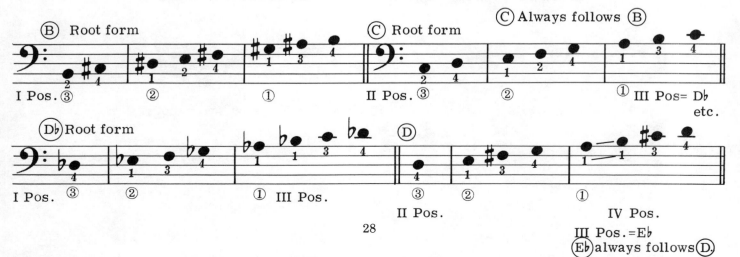

28

Major Chords

We can derive a major chord by using the 1st, 3rd, and 5th notes of the scale.

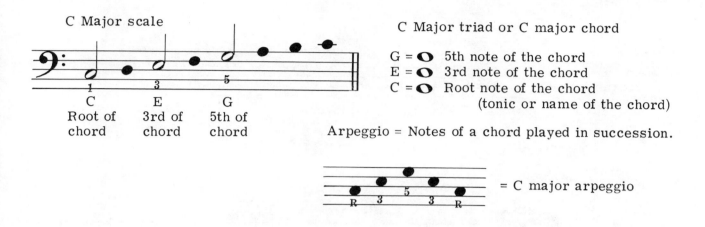

If you have studied your scales, you will find the construction in memorization of chords quite easy as they are always built using every other letter of the alphabet.
Example: A B C D E G A B C D E F G A

Any "A" chord will have the letters A, C, E, with the appropriate sharps and flats.
Any "E" chord will have the letters E, G, B, with the appropriate sharps and flats.
Learn this principle now and save countless hours of frustration when building more complex harmonies. Build some chords using the major scales.
Remember - chords (Every other letter of the alphabet.)

The Major Chord Arpeggios in the First Position

29

Inversions

When we build a chord from the root we call it root position.
When we build a chord from the 3rd letter of the chord, we call it the 1st inversion.
When we build a chord from the 5th letter of the chord, we call it the 2nd inversion.
The lowest sounding note of the chord determines its inversion.

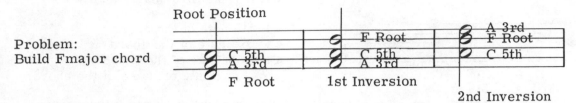

Problem:
Build Fmajor chord

Suggested Ways of Practicing

Ⓒ major scale, Ⓒ arpeggio + inversions

Play this pattern through all major keys.

Must be played daily and memorized.

After the chords become more familiar, practice playing the complete arpeggios starting with
the lowest note of the chord found in the 1st position - Example: C major (C E G)
The lowest sound is the letter E on the 4th string.
Start the chord arpeggio on the note E and continue the arpeggio until you reach the highest
sound in the 1st position which is the note G.

30

Memorizing major scales, spelling of chords, and the ability to play these arpeggios in all inversions is a big step in building a firm foundation that will carry you far in bass guitar development.

More 1/16 Note Rhythms

In order to understand the rhythm it is wise to count aloud. say "1" while playing the note G, then say "a" to represent the remaining time value left in the note before playing the next note G which starts on the "and". If you do not say the "a" you will have a tendency to rush the first note G and not give it the full value which is 2/16 or 1/8 (the complete down of your foot).

Remember to count aloud and be sure to say the last "a" on the upbeat in order to insure the 1/8 note having its full value.

1/16 Note Drill

Key Signatures

A key signature is an artificial device placed at the beginning of a piece. It tells the performer which note to sharp or flat. Key signatures are derived from the scale. (Key = Scale)

Memorize this chart

Notice that the sharp keys are five letters apart from each other.
Notice that the sharps are five letters apart from each other.
Notice that the flat keys are four letters apart from each other.
Notice that the flats are four letters apart from each other.

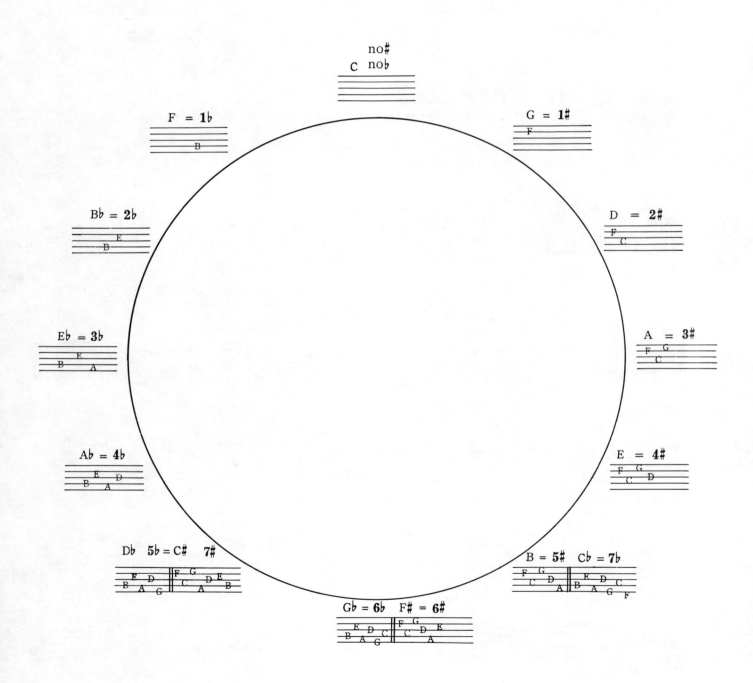

32

Intervals

An interval is the distance between two notes measured in half and whole steps. There are five kinds of intervals to be studied.

Perfect = P   Major = M   Minor = m   Augmented = A   Diminished = D

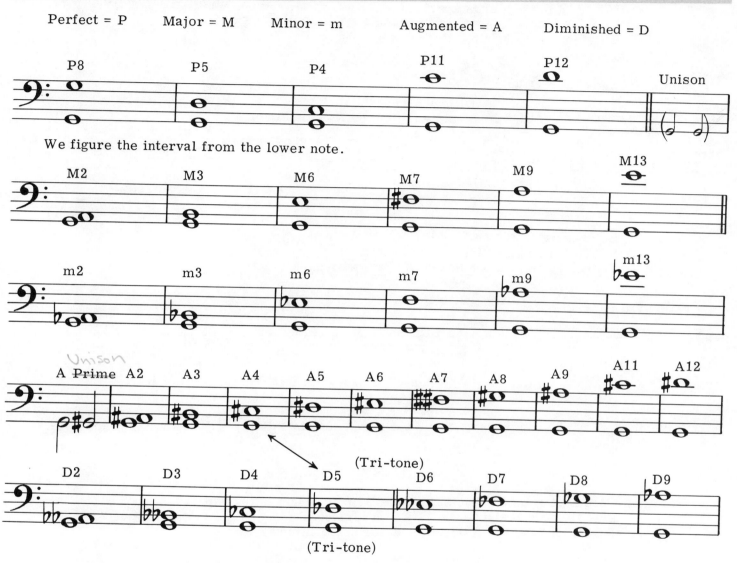

We figure the interval from the lower note.

(Tri-tone)

(Tri-tone)

Compound intervals are larger than an octave. Memorize this chart.
Many intervals are enharmonic but are named by the letters involved. The following chart should be thoroughly understood before proceeding.

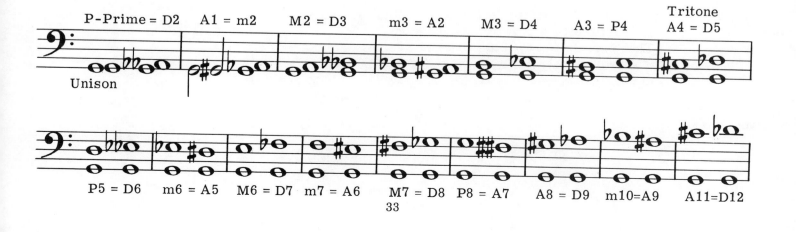

Major 3rds and Minor 3rds
(Intervallic Construction)

Construction; A major 3rd consists of 3 letters and 4 frets (use the alphabet to help you)

        A B C D E F G A B C

Problem: Construct a major 3rd on the note D - (alphabet A B C D̄ E F̄ G)

        D to F is three letters apart (in other words, every other letter)

        Play the note D open string and add 4 frets - 4th fret F#

        Therefore D to F# = 3 letters and 4 frets, a major 3rd.

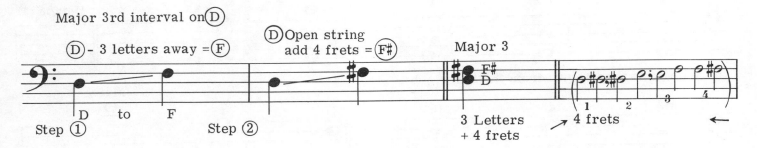

Problem: Build a major 3rd on B♭ - B to D is 3 letters apart.

        B♭, (1st fret) add 4 frets = D 5th fret

        Therefore B♭ to D = 3 letters and 4 frets, a major 3rd.

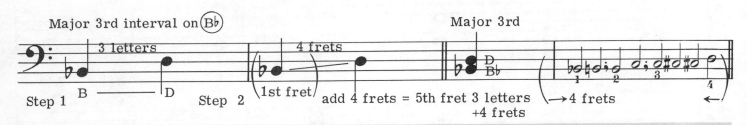

Remember - Step 1 is important, you must use every other letter of the alphabet, then figure your fret distance.

Problem: Construct a minor 3rd on the note D. D to F is 3 letters apart.

        Play the note D and add 3 frets = 3rd fret, F.

        Therefore D to F = 3 letters and 3 frets, a minor 3rd.

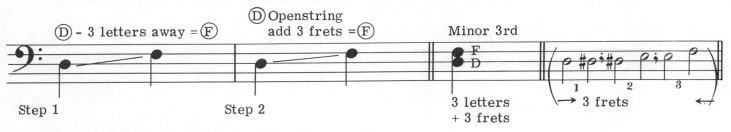

Problem: Build a minor 3rd on B♭ - B to D is 3 letters apart.

        B♭, (1st fret) add 3 frets = D♭ 4th fret.

        Therefore B♭ to D♭ = 3 letters and 3 frets, A minor 3rd.

Notice that the difference between a major and minor 3rd is the difference of 1 less fret, however, the letters remain the same for both the major and minor 3rd. Ex. A♭ to C = M3; A♭ to C♭ = m3 (not B)

Build major 3rd intervals on the following notes.

Learn to sing and hear this major 3rd interval.

Formula #1

Notice that these notes are in the same order as the major key signatures.

Build minor 3rd intervals on the following notes.

Learn to sing and hear this minor 3rd interval.

Formula #2

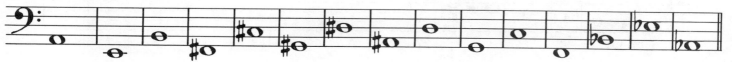

Notice that the C major triad has a major & minor 3rd interval.

C major = maj3 + min 3

Review your triads by constructing major triads on formula #1 using the M3 & m3 interval method.

Therefore, A major triad is composed of a major 3rd & a minor 3rd.

The 4 minor scales. (pure, harmonic, classic melodic, jazz melodic)

1) The pure minor scale can be formed by starting from the 6th note of A major scale to the 6th note one octave higher using the notes of that major scale.
Notice that the D minor scale uses only notes of the F major scale.
Notice that it has the same flat note (B♭)

The D minor scale is known as the relative minor to F major scale.
It has the same signature (1 flat - B♭)
Play the scale and notice the modal sound. You can recognize it as the aeolian mode discussed earlier in the chapter on major scales + modes.

2) After forming the scale, notice that the half steps occur between the 2 - 3, 5 - 6 notes of the scale.

Problem: construct the E pure minor scale

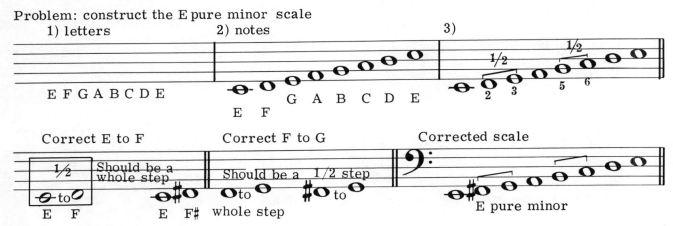

3) A third way to form the scale is to lower the 3rd, 6th, and 7th notes of the major scale.

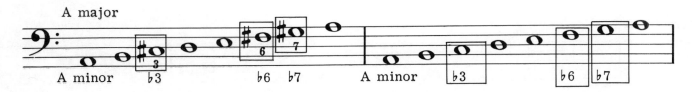

On the notes of formula 2 construct minor scales using the 3 methods outlined above. The following is a list of pure minor scales. Play ascending and descending.

36

Dotted 1/8 and 1/16 Notes

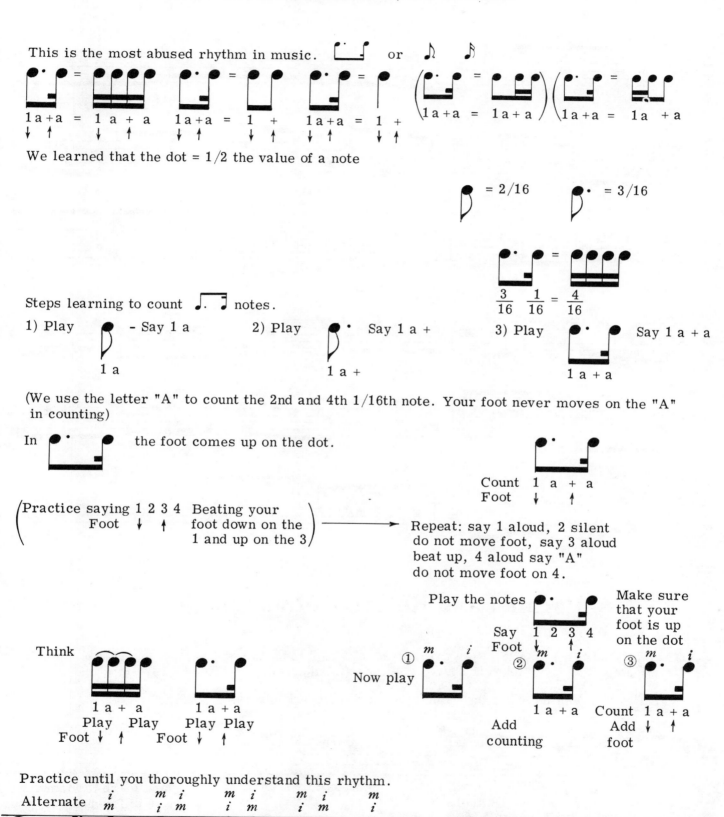

This is the most abused rhythm in music.

We learned that the dot = 1/2 the value of a note

$$\frac{3}{16} \quad \frac{1}{16} = \frac{4}{16}$$

Steps learning to count notes.

1) Play — Say 1 a   2) Play — Say 1 a +   3) Play — Say 1 a + a

(We use the letter "A" to count the 2nd and 4th 1/16th note. Your foot never moves on the "A" in counting)

In the foot comes up on the dot.

Count 1 a + a
Foot   ↓   ↑

Practice saying 1 2 3 4 Beating your
        Foot ↓   ↑   foot down on the
                        1 and up on the 3

Repeat: say 1 aloud, 2 silent
do not move foot, say 3 aloud
beat up, 4 aloud say "A"
do not move foot on 4.

Play the notes   Make sure
                      that your
Say 1 2 3 4   foot is up
Foot ↓   ↑   on the dot

Think

1 a + a   1 a + a
Play Play   Play Play
Foot ↓ ↑   Foot ↓ ↑

Now play ①   ② Add counting   ③ Count 1 a + a
                  1 a + a   Add ↓ ↑
                                           foot

Practice until you thoroughly understand this rhythm.

Alternate

Count 1 a + a   2 a + a   3 a + a   4 a + a
Foot   ↓   ↑   ↓   ↑   ↓   ↑   ↓   ↑

37

Dotted 1/8 and 1/16 Exercise

Alternate   *i*   *m*   *i*   *m*

Count aloud
Foot

Parallel and Relative Minor Scale

C major and C minor are called parallel major and minor scales. Both scales use the same letter notes but have different sharps and flats (In other words, different key signatures)

(C major and A minor have the same # + ♭ but different letters)

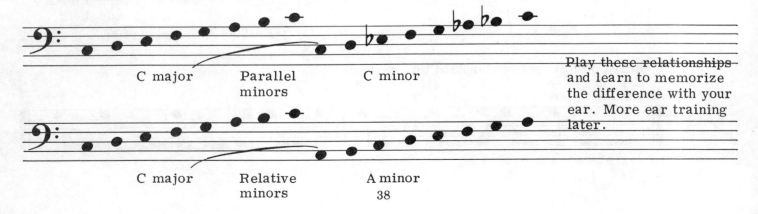

C major   Parallel   C minor
           minors

Play these relationships and learn to memorize the difference with your ear. More ear training later.

C major   Relative   A minor
           minors

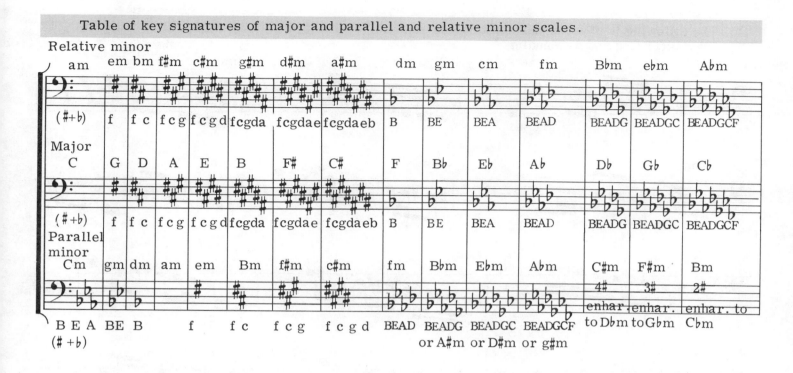

The Harmonic Minor Scale

1) Construction - Write the pure minor scale and raise the 7th note one fret.

The "A" pure minor scale   The "A" harmonic minor scale

Double sharp sign

g#minor pure   The g# harmonic minor scale

2) Construction - Write a major scale and lower the 3rd and 6th notes.

F major   F harmonic

3) Notice the half steps between (2 - 3,) (5 - 6,) (7 - 8) notes. Also notice the 1-1/2 steps between 6th and 7th notes.

Construct harmonic scales on the notes in formula 2 and use the major scale and half step methods.

The following is a list of harmonic minor scales.
Play ascending and descending.

Play your major pure, and harmonic scales daily until you obtain speed and memorize them.
Always play using alternate fingering, with volume, and keep your fingers down until you
change strings.
Learn to recognize the 3 scales by ear.

The Classic Melodic Minor Scale

Construction: Play the pure minor scale and raise the 6th and 7th notes one fret when ascending
and lower the 6th and 7th notes when descending.

Pure minor   Classic melodic minor

Student should construct the classic melodic scales on formula 2. (Notice that the descending
classic melodic scale is the same as a pure minor scale.)

The following is a list of classic melodic minor scales:

The Jazz Melodic Minor Scale

Construction: 1) This scale is formed by raising the 6th and 7th notes of the pure minor scale ascending and descending.
(Another name for the pure minor is natural minor.)

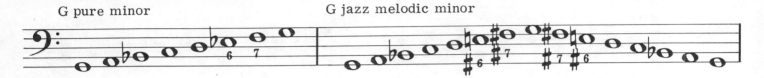

2) Play a major scale and lower the 3rd note.

The student must construct the scales on formula 2.
The following is a list of Jazz melodic minor scales. Play ascending and descending.

At this point we must: 1) Start singing and hearing scales daily to be able to recognize them by sound.
2) Play them daily in the first position sparing no pains to memorize them with speed, volume and a good tone.
There is no chapter in music which is more neglected than the complete study of minor scales especially in the early training of most students. The jazz melodic minor scale is one of the most important scales you can work with as you will discover in your later training with modes.

Triplets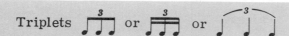

A triplet is a 3 note figure played in the same value of time as a 2 note figure using the same note values.

Think of a 3 syllable word when you count triplets. Hap-pi-ly, mer-ri-ly

Say hap-pi-ly

An 1/8 note triplet = 1 beat.
Do not worry about the up of the foot or the "and" when counting.

Count 1 = 1

We can also use the alternating stroke.

Notice that the m finger is used in repeating motion between each triplet.
It helps to count the triplet if you accent the 1st note of the triplet figure.

Accent mark

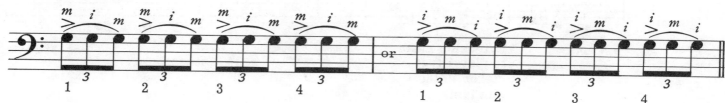

Triplet Exercise

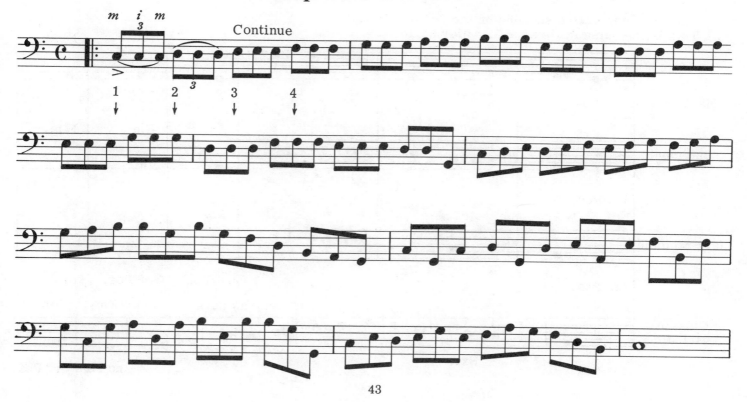

A few 1st position moveable forms of minor scales.

After memorizing these forms, move them up and down the fingerboard keeping the same finger patterns throughout. Use the fret guide.

Start on root or name of the scale.

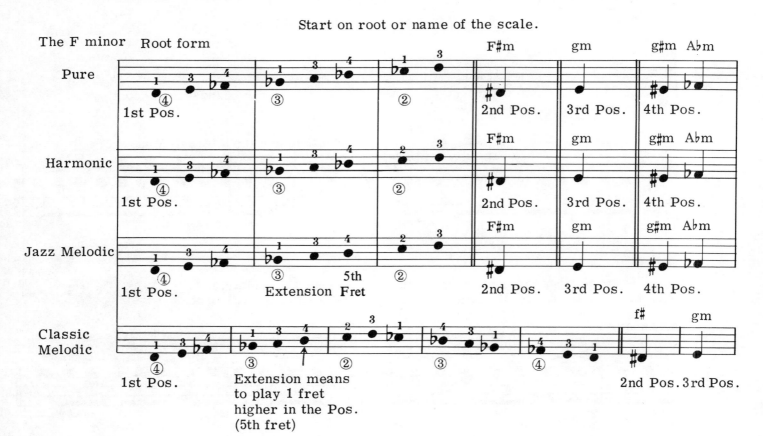

The F minor   Root form

Pure

Harmonic

Jazz Melodic

Classic
Melodic

Extension means
to play 1 fret
higher in the Pos.
(5th fret)

The E♭ minor scales starting on the 3rd of the scale.
This is the same scale as a G♭ major scale.

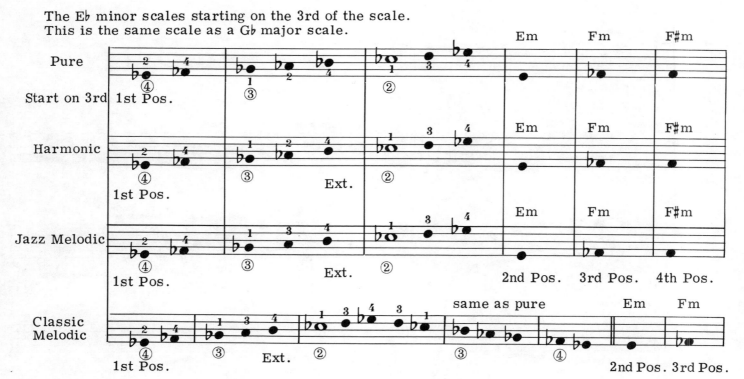

44

The B♭m scales starting on the 5th note of the scale

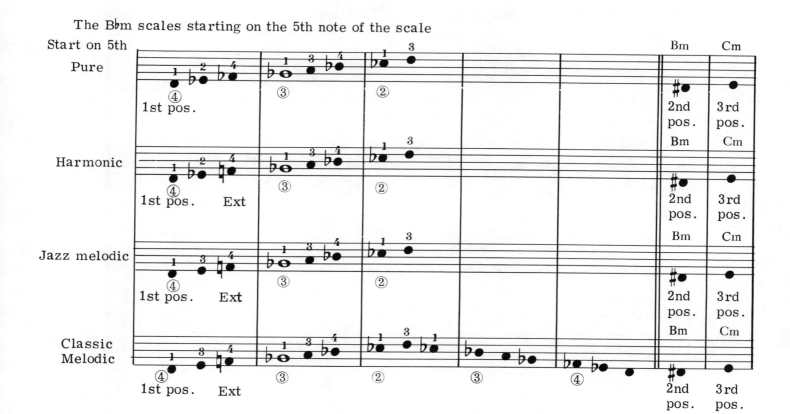

The A♭ minor scales starting on the root

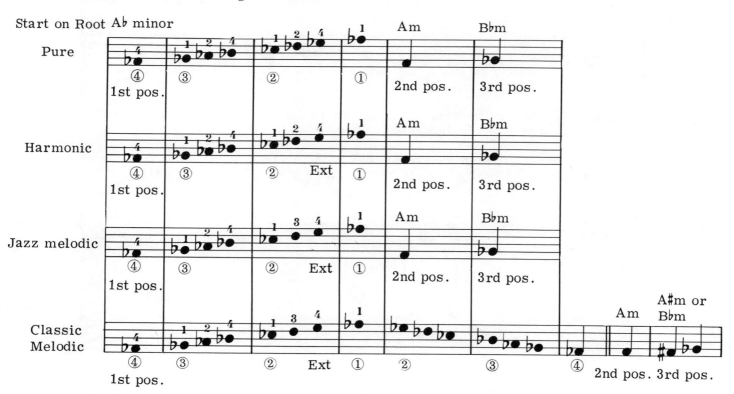

Remember, we are learning to play all the scales and arpeggios from the lowest sound in the position to improve our ideas and technical proficiency that we will need later playing lines and ideas.

Minor Triads

1) Play a major scale and extract 1 and ♭3, and 5 from the scale.
Notice every other letter of the alphabet is used.

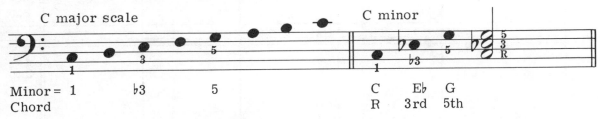

Minor = 1   ♭3   5   C   E♭   G
Chord   R   3rd   5th

2) Play any minor scale form and extract 1, 3, 5 from the scale.

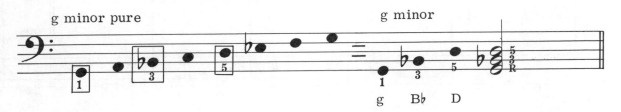

                                     g   B♭   D

3) Build a minor triad using intervals.
a minor triad is composed of a minor 3rd and major 3rd.

      Problem: Construct D minor
        D+ F = minor 3rd -   F to A + major 3rd   D minor

Review the chapter on major and minor 3rds and build minor triads on the notes in formula 2 using intervals as well as the 2 scale methods above.

Minor chord arpeggios starting on the lowest note of the chord.
(*) This is known as a hold or fermata - it means to hold the note a few counts longer.

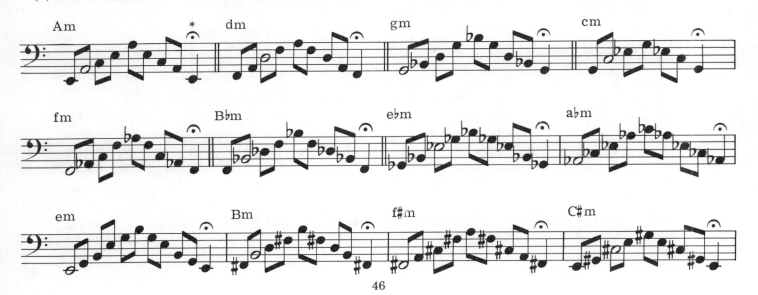

After playing these arpeggios, learn to play them from their root positions as follows.

Notice the comparison between major + minor triads

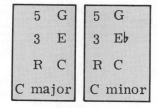

1) The letters are always the same.
2) The middle note (the 3rd of the chord) is always 1 fret lower.
3) To form a minor 3rd from a major 3rd, lower the 3rd 1 fret.
4) To form a major 3rd from a minor 3rd, raise the 3rd 1 fret.

The names of the degree notes of the major scale.

Every note of the major and minor scales is called a degree and has a technical name.

1) Tonic
2) Super tonic
3) Mediant
4) Sub dominant
5) Dominant
6) Sub mediant
7) Leading tone   memorize these.

C major

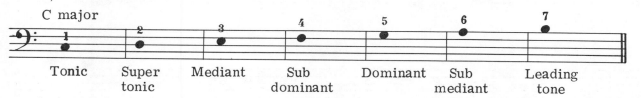

The Dominant 7th Scale, Chord, and Arpeggio
The Dominant 7th Scale

Construction: 1) Play from the 5th note of a major scale to the 5th note of that scale one octave higher.

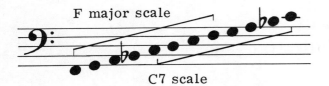

The C7 scale is called the C dominant scale or the C mixolydian mode.

Notice that the dominant scale is the same scale as the mixolydian scale.

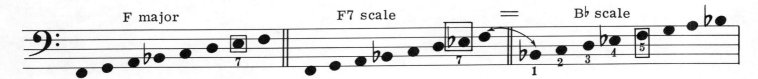

By lowering the 7th of a major scale, we form a dominant 7th scale. Notice that the mixolydian scale starting on F has two flats. (same scale as the Bb major scale.)
F is the dominant note in the key of Bb (The 5th note of the Bb scale)

The following is a list of dominant 7th scales.

Remember, dominant scale = Mixolydian mode. These are mixolydian modes.

48

The Dominant 7th Chord

The dominant 7th chord is built using the 1, 3, 5, ♭7 of the major scale. Notice every other letter of the alphabet.

Intervallic construction:

A dominant 7th is composed of (a major 3rd, minor 3rd) , and minor 3rd.
(a major chord)

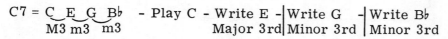

C7 = C E G B♭ - Play C - Write E -|Write G - |Write B♭
M3 m3 m3   Major 3rd|Minor 3rd|Minor 3rd

Maj.3   Min.3   Min.3

On the formula I notes build dominant 7th chords with 1) Intervals
2) Scale construction.

Ex. 1) Intervallic

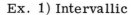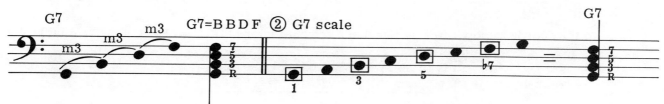

The following is a list of dominant 7th arpeggios. (Memorize)

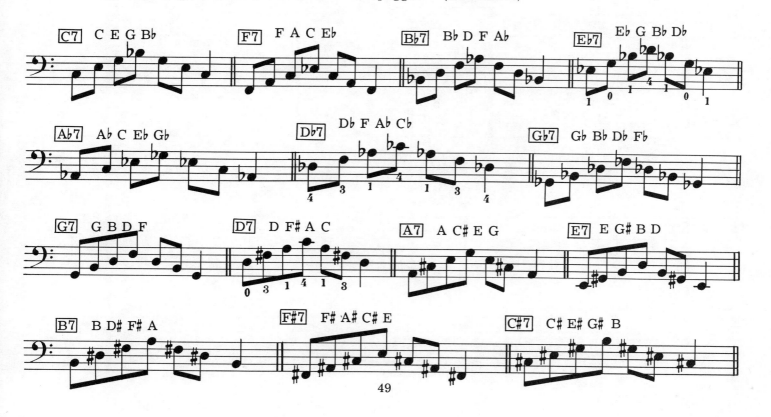

Dominant 7th to Tonic Progression

Most dominant 7th chords will resolve (move) to their major and minor tonics. This progression is called V7 to I. The dominant 7th chord has the same notes whether it is in F major or F harmonic minor.

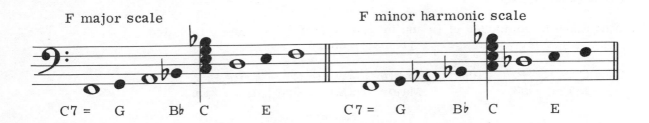

Both of these C7 chords are formed from these parallel F major and F harmonic minor scales. Both C7 chords resolve to their respective tonic chords. (C7 to F) (C7 to F minor)

The following is a list of (V7 to I) in major and minor keys.
Learn these progressions as they appear in practically every tune.

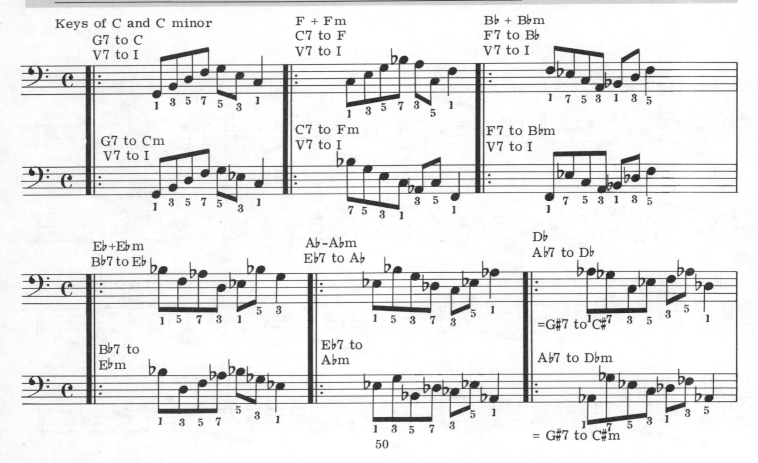

50

What we are trying to do is to learn to play the dominant 7th and tonic chords in any inversion.

G7 - G B D F = Root position
     B D F G = 1st inv.
     D F G B = 2nd inv.
     F G B D = 3rd inv.

51

V7 to I Bass Patterns

The following is a list of bass figures that can be played when the V7 to I progression is written. The bassist need not play all the notes of the written harmonies. The root and 5th are the best sounding notes unless other notes are specifically asked for.

It is obvious that there are many combinations. The student should play V7 - I progressions in different keys.

In order to play more melodic bass lines, the bassist adds the other chord notes or scale notes.

There are many combinations and the student should look for them using different V7 to I progressions.

A few 1st position moveable dominant 7th arpeggio forms.

Root form

Form 3 - Starts on the 3rd of the chord

Form 5 - Starts on the 5th of the chord

Form 7 - Starts on the 7th of the chord

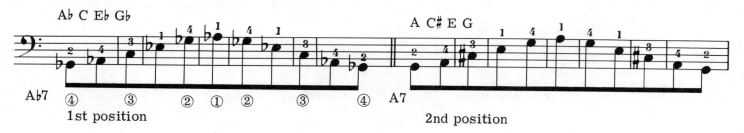

Root form

Play these moveable forms up and down the fingerboard.
Memorize, play with volume and speed and alternate fingering.

The student most be able to sing, hear, and play major, minor and dominant 7th scales and arpeggios.
The following is a suggested way of practicing scales:
Take any note and play all six scales ascending and descending.
Play with volume, correct hand attack and memorize.

Start with F

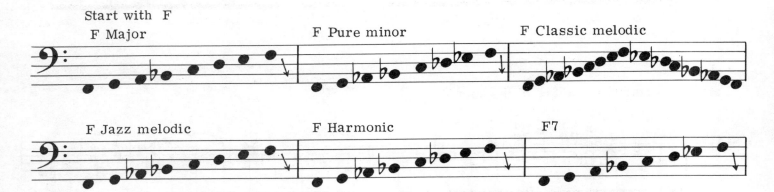

Each day start with a new key striving for a good connected sound.

Arpeggio exercise of major, minor, and dominant 7th arpeggios

Try to develop speed and memorization of this valuable exercise.

The Blues Scale

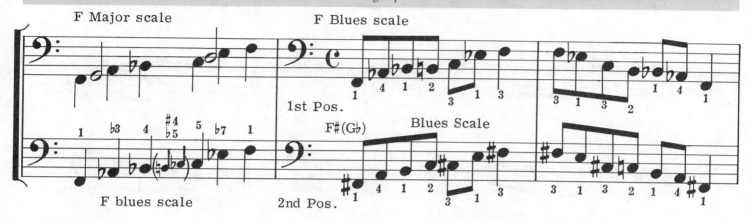

Student is to construct all blues scales on the major scales learned.

The fifteen blues scales in the cycle of Fifths

Play ascending and descending
Play slowly at first then gain speed and memorize.
There are only 12 keys but we write 15 to expose the student to reading multiple sharp and flat keys.

The 12 blues scales in chromatic sequence with rhythmical patterns.

1) These are difficult but are worth practicing for rhythm training.
2) Sing and count aloud when playing.

Syncopation

Broadly speaking by syncopation we mean a displacement of natural accents.

The 1st and 3rd beat are the strongest.
The 2nd and 4th beat are weaker.

When we play a note on a weaker beat and hold that sound through a stronger beat, we produce syncopation.
G is played on the 2nd beat and held through the stronger 3rd beat.

The "and" of the 3rd beat is played and held through the 4th stronger beat.

Any down "beat" is stronger than any "up" beat.

Syncopation Exercise

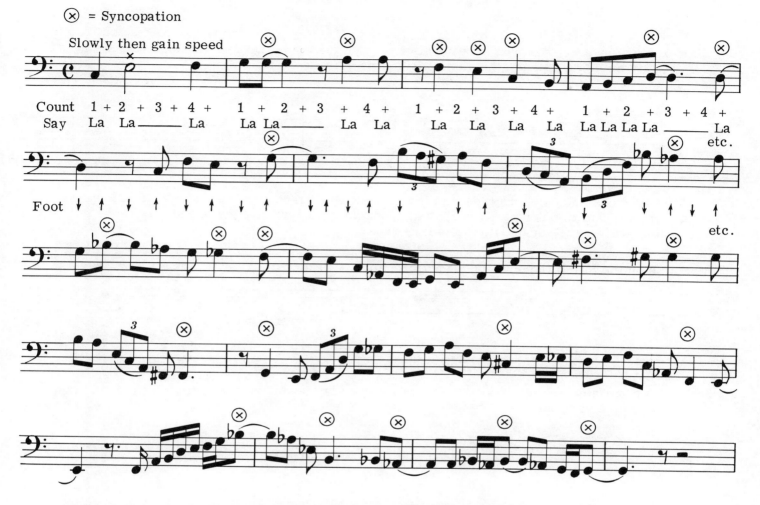

This is difficult but will become easy if it is practiced in the following manner.
1) Say the rhythms counting aloud using the syllable "La"
2) Play the rhythms counting aloud
3) Play the rhythms counting to yourself.

Blues in Syncopation

The II Position

The II position means to place the 1st finger on the 2nd fret, the 2nd finger on the 3rd fret, the 3rd finger on the 4th fret, and the 4th finger on the 5th fret. (The 4th finger can be called on to play the 6th fret known as an extension fingering.)

(G) Major II Pos. scale and arpeggio

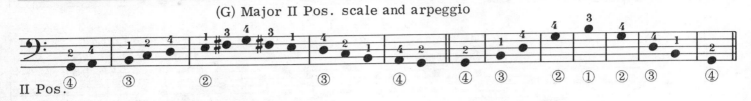

This is a movable scale and arpeggio. By moving all fingers up 1 fret and keeping the same pattern, we play the Ab III pos. scale and arpeggio. Use your fret guide and play these movable scales+arp. up and down the fingerboard.

(Starts on the 3rd of the scale)   D Major   scale + arpeggio

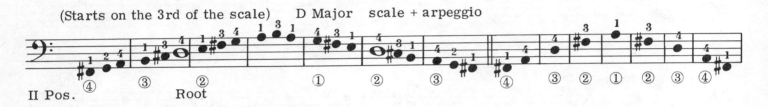

This is a movable scale - III pos. = Eb scale+arp. Play up and down the fingerboard with the help of your fret guide.

A Major   scale + arpeggio

Again these are movable scales + arpeggios. III pos. = Bb scale + arp. The following 4 minor, mixolydian and blues scales are movable and should be played up and down the fingerboard.

F# minor scales + arpeggios

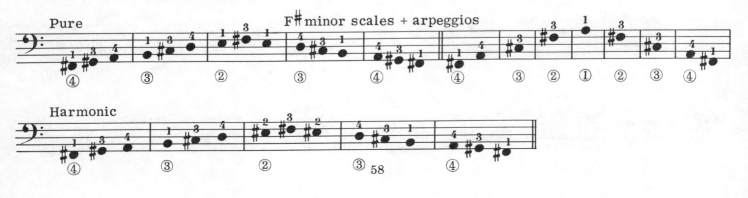

58

59

4 Movable dominant 7th scales & arpeggios in IIpos.

A7

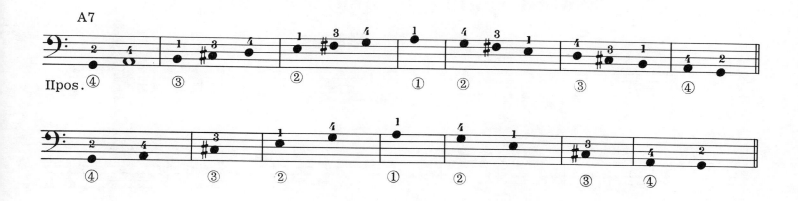

IIpos. ④   ③   ②   ①   ②   ③   ④

④   ③   ②   ①   ②   ③   ④

F# blues scale in II pos.

IIpos. ④   ③   ②   ③   ④

Notice that we have learned 3 modes in the II pos; the ionian (major), the aeolian (pure minor), and the mixolydian (Dom.7th). Play all scales ascending & descending up and down the finger board, (alternate fingering), (fingers down), volume.

II Position Notes

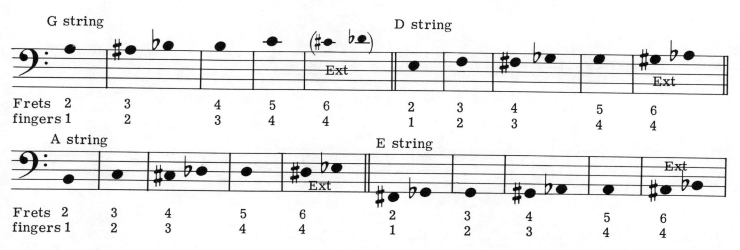

G string					D string				
Frets 2	3	4	5	6	2	3	4	5	6
fingers 1	2	3	4	4	1	2	3	4	4

A string					E string				
Frets 2	3	4	5	6	2	3	4	5	6
fingers 1	2	3	4	4	1	2	3	4	4

In order to learn to read fluently throughout the fingerboard all notes must be instantly recognized regarding their fret and string locations. The good reader knows where to play any pitch in different areas of the bass. This is what leads to good fingerings and excellent sight reading ability.

Note Reading in the II Position

Use the scale patterns to help you to read the exercise above.
Write in the fingering lightly, then erase it after a few practices.
After you learn this exercise you should know half the fingerboard.

Blues Patterns in I and II Positions

The Whole Tone Scale, Chord, and Arpeggio

The whole tone consists of 6 notes, one whole step apart from each other.
(two frets)

It is a symmetrical scale because all the notes in the scale are equidistant from each other. (2 frets apart)

There are only 2 different whole tone scales.
They can be built from any 2 consecutive chromatic notes.

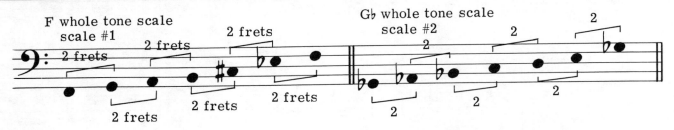

Scale #1 -------- F   G   A   B   C♯   E♭   F

Chromatic scale	F	(F♯/G♭)	G	(G♯/A♭)	A	(B♭/A♯)	B	C	(C♯/D♭)	D	(D♯/E♭)	E	F

Scale #2 -------- Gb   Ab   Bb   C   D   E   Gb

No matter which note of scale #1 you start on you will have the same pattern scale because all notes are equidistant, 2 frets away from each other. This applies to scale #2.

Whole Tone Scale Exercises

Whole tone position forms in the I and II positions

Notice the ease in shifting positions when you shift on an open string. Remember this valuable weapon as you progress up the fingerboard.

The augmented chord (augmented = Aug. or (+))

Construction: 1) Play every other note of the whole tone scale.

The F whole tone scale generates the F+ chord and the G+ chord

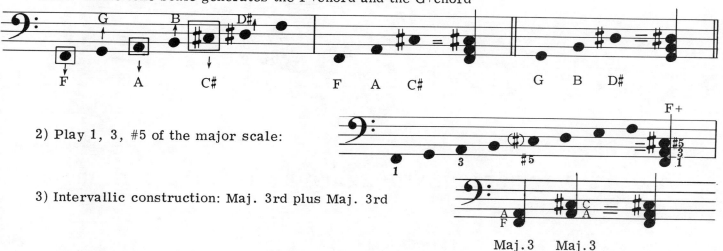

2) Play 1, 3, #5 of the major scale:

3) Intervallic construction: Maj. 3rd plus Maj. 3rd

Notice every other letter in the spelling of the chord.
Notice that the whole tone scale generates 2 aug. chords.

There are 2 different augmented scales each generating 2 different augmented chords which means that there are 4 different aug. chords. Each chord has 3 names because the chord is an equal interval chord and the notes of the chord are a major 3rd apart.

Scale #1

Scale #1 (F+ chord = F A C# or A C# E# or Db F A (3 chords)
G+ chord = G B D# or B D# (F##/G) or (Eb/D#) G B (3 chords)

Scale #2

Scale #2 Gb+ chord = Gb Bb D or Bb D (F#/Gb) or D F# (A#/Bb) (3 chords)
Ab+ chord = Ab C E or C E (G#/Ab) or E (G#/Ab) (B#/C) (3 chords)

There are 2 different whole tone scales and 4 different aug. chords. Learn to spell, sing, and hear these sounds.
Take any 4 consecutive chromatic notes and build 4 different aug. chords. Take any 2 consecutive chromatic notes and build 2 different aug. scales.

The 12 Augmented Scales in the 1st Position

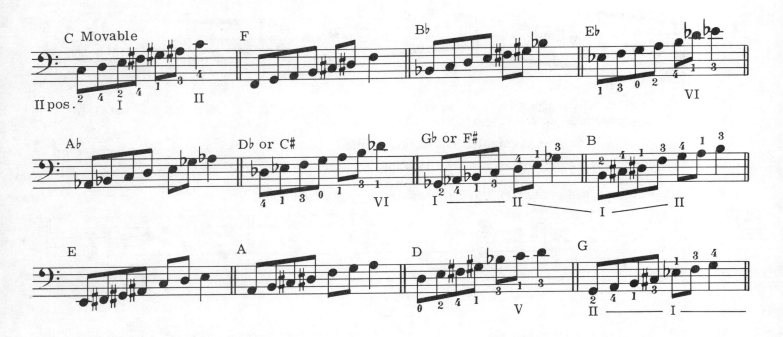

The 12 Augmented Arpeggios in the I-II Position

Remember each augmented arpeggio = 3 arpeggio spellings Ex: C+= C E G♯ and E G♯ B♯ and A♭ C E There are 4 diff. arpeggios notated 3 ways = 12 different arpeggios.

Whole Tone Arpeggio Patterns

In future scale construction, remember the word augmented usually will refer to the 5th note of a chord.

III Position Notes on 4 Strings

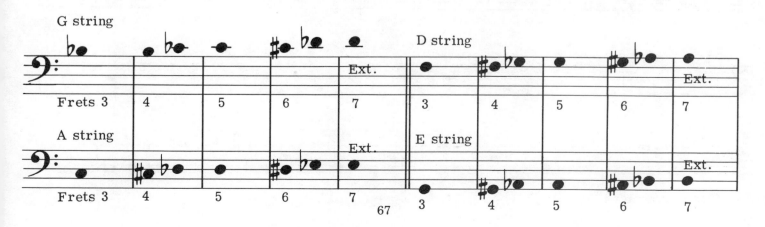

Note Reading Exercise in the III Position

All notes are to be played in the III pos. (3-4-5-6 frets)

3rd fret   4th fret   5th fret   6th fret

7 fret extensions

Diminished Scales, Chords, and Arpeggios

There are 2 kinds of diminished scales we will be studying:

The whole - Half diminished scale (Whole = W) (Diminished = dim. or(0))
(Half   = H)

> Construction: Start on any note and play a note 2 frets away, then play a note 1 fret away.
> Continue this pattern of 2 frets - 1 fret etc.
> We use many enharmonics in diminished spellings. The rule is: What is easy to read is usually correct.

C diminished W - H step scale

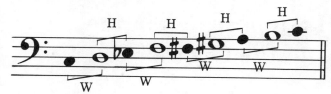

F diminished (W-H) scale

Fingering
1   3   4   1   2   4   0   2   3

Play ascending and descending

Scale #1 starting on the note F

There are 3 different W - H step dim. scales.
Write any 3 consecutive chromatic notes and construct the W - H step dim. scales.
Each scale will have 4 different names and this produces our 12 scales.
The 1st, 3rd, 5th and 7th note each names a different scale.

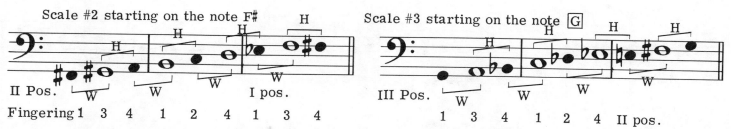

Scale #2 starting on the note F♯

II Pos.

Fingering 1   3   4   1   2   4   1   3   4

Scale #3 starting on the note G

III Pos.

1   3   4   1   2   4   II pos.

We used the 3 notes F, F♯, G, to form our 3 different scales. If we had used the notes G♯ or A♭, we would have formed the same scale pattern notes as F dim. Scale #1 except we would have started on the 3rd note of that F dim. scale #1. Instead of starting on the note F♯, we could have started on the note A and this would have produced the same notes as scale #2 starting on F♯. If we started on the note B♭, we would have repeated the same pattern as the notes of scale #3 starting on the note G. What we are saying is that every 3rd note will give us a new name for the scale but actually the same pattern sound scale. (Refer to the circled notes in the following diagrammed scale)

F Dim Scale

Ab Dim Scale

B° Dim Scale

F°scale=Ab°scale=B° scale=D° scale

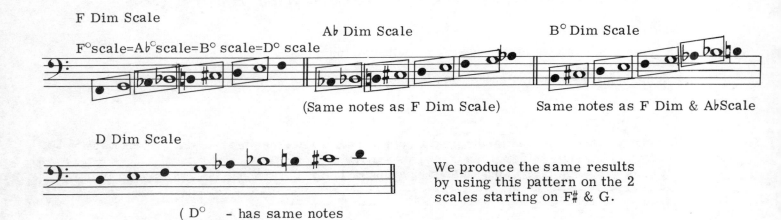

(Same notes as F Dim Scale)

Same notes as F Dim & AbScale

D Dim Scale

We produce the same results
by using this pattern on the 2
scales starting on F# & G.

(D° - has same notes
as Fdim, Ab dim, & B dim scales)

The 12 Diminished W−H Step Scales in the
I−II−III Positions in the Cycle

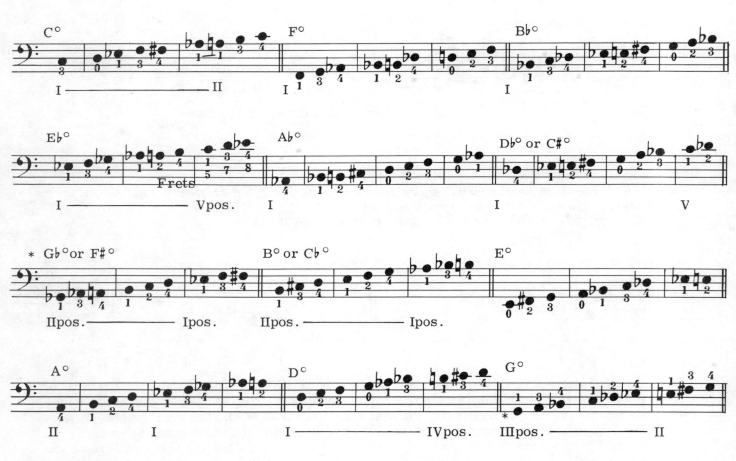

* Notice the (F#°) and G° scale fingerings. This 2 position fingering is worthy of memorization.
  (Gb°)

It is an easy movable pattern that should be played throughout the fingerboard. Play all scales
ascending and descending; practice singing & hearing.

The H - W step diminished scale.

Construction: Play a note, write a note 1 fret away then write another note 2 frets away.
Continue this pattern of 1 fret, 2 frets.

There are 3 (H - W) dim. Scales. Each is spelled 4 ways.
Use any 3 consecutive chromatic notes and form the 3 different (H - W) step dim. Scales.

Everything that applies to the (W - H) step dim. scale applies to the (H - W) dim. scales.
By starting on every 3rd note of the scale we repeat the scale pattern sounds and actually
have the same scale.

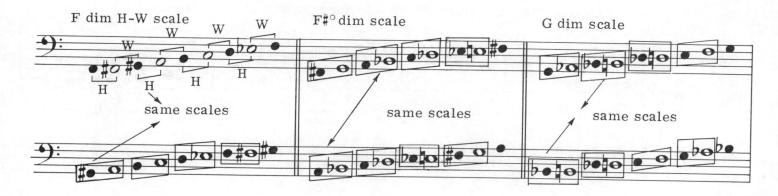

The 12 H – W Step Diminished Scales in the Cycle

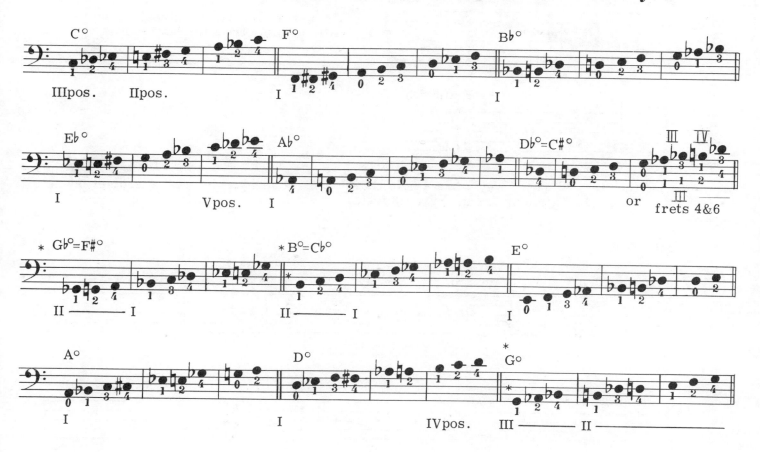

* These 3 two position scales should be memorized.

71

W - H moveable diminished scale pattern (2 position scale)

4 string

The moveable 3 position H - W step diminished scale on 4 strings

Notice that we need 3 positions to finger the scale.
Play these 2 scales up and down the finger board.

The diminished 7th chord and arpeggio
Construction: 1) Play every other note of either dim. scale.

W-H scale

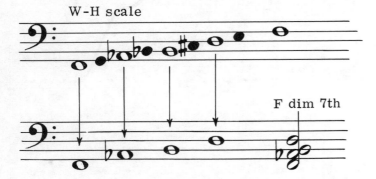

F dim 7th

We do not concern ourselves
with the dim. triad for jazz sounds.

We use the dim. 7th chord which is a 4 note chord. This is an equal interval chord, every note
being separated by a minor 3rd interval - (3 frets)

Construction

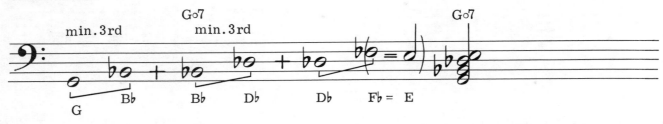

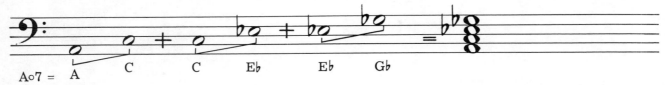

72

There are 3 dim. 7th chords - each is spelled 4 ways.

Take any 3 consecutive chromatic notes and build 3 dim. 7th chords.

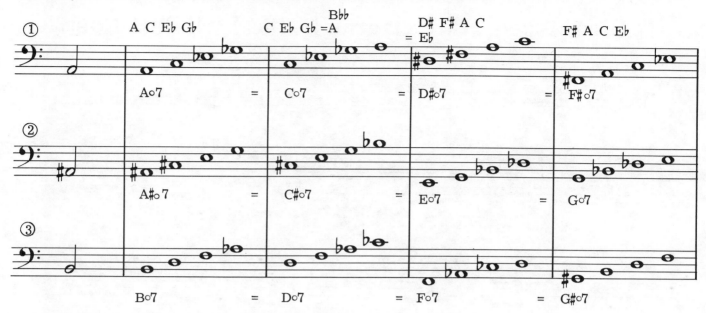

Play these arpeggios to hear what you write.

The 12 diminished 7th arpeggios; sing, hear, and play.

There are 3 different dim. (W - H) and (H - W) scales and 3 different dim. 7th chords and arpeggios each spelled 4 ways. Remember, each different dim. Scale is repeated on every 3rd note of that scale.

Diminished 7th Patterns in the I − II − III Positions

New Chords to be Memorized

1) Major 7th - Play the 1, 3, 5, 7 notes of the major scale.
   - Play a major chord and add a major 3rd interval.

Construct major 7th chords intervallically and scalewise
On formula #1

The 12 major 7th arpeggios in the 1st +2nd pos.

Memorize these chords + learn to sing and hear them; play the arpeggios with the asterisks using 1st pos. fingerings, then play the movable finger patterns up+down the fingerboard.

5 Movable Major 7th Forms

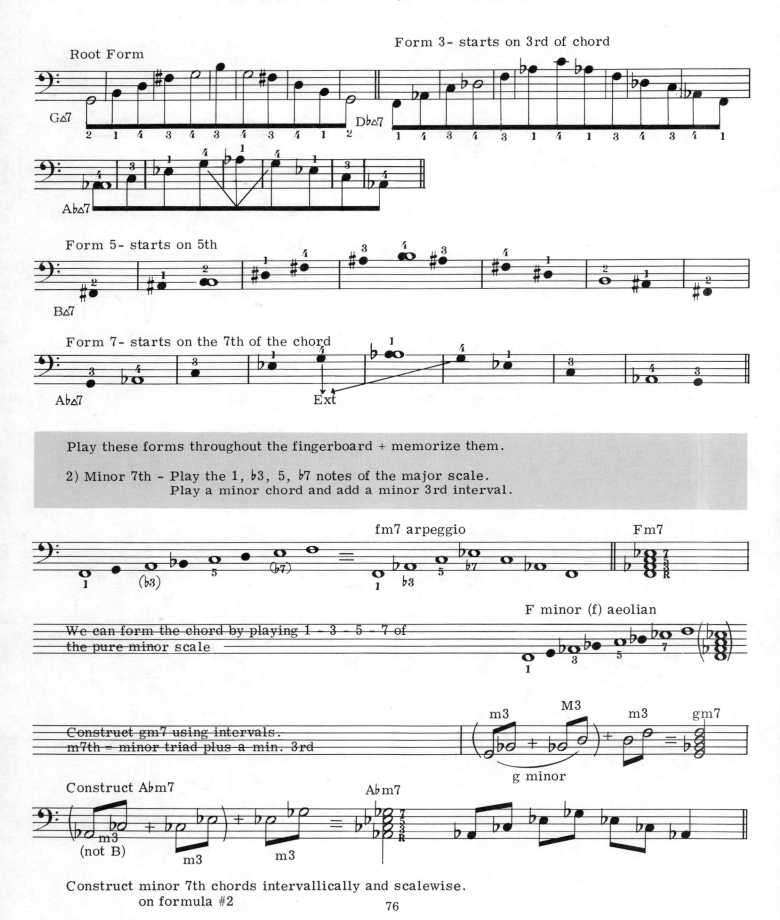

Play these forms throughout the fingerboard + memorize them.

2) Minor 7th - Play the 1, ♭3, 5, ♭7 notes of the major scale.
   Play a minor chord and add a minor 3rd interval.

We can form the chord by playing 1 - 3 - 5 - 7 of the pure minor scale

Construct gm7 using intervals.
m7th = minor triad plus a min. 3rd

Construct A♭m7

Construct minor 7th chords intervallically and scalewise.
   on formula #2

76

The 12 Minor 7th Arpeggios in the I Position and I — III Position Forms

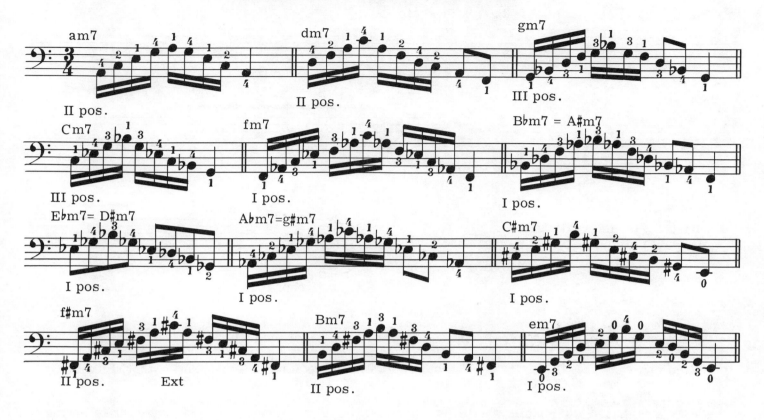

5 Movable Min. 7th Forms

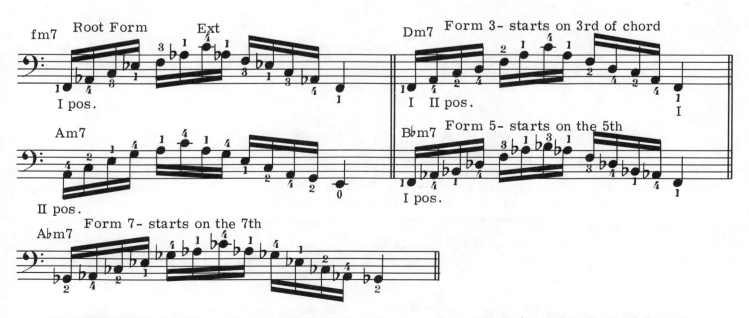

Memorize and play throughout the fingerboard; as you play pattern fingerings up and down the fingerboard, try to think notes instead of numbers.

The Major 6th Chord

Construction: Play 1 3 5 6 of the major scale

F major

F6 = F A C D

Construct G6 intervallically
Major 6th = (maj. chord plus maj. 2nd)

G6 = G B D E

G maj. chord

Construct major 6th chords scalewise + intervallically on formula #1

Notice that C6 = C E G A
Notice that Am7 = A C E G
} Both chords have the same letters. Notice that C major and A minor are relative maj. & minor.

Rule = Any major 6th contains the same notes as its relative minor 7th: memorize the following M6 & m7 relationships.

C6 = Am7 = C6	G6 = Em7 = G6	Learn to spell the relationships both ways -
F6 = Dm7 = F6	D6 = Bm7 = D6	(maj. 6 to min. 7)+(min. 7 to maj. 6)
Bb6 = Gm7 = Bb6	A6 = f#m7 = A6	
Eb6 = Cm7 = Eb6	E6 = C#m7 = E6	
Ab6 = fm7 = Ab6	B6 = g#m7 = B6	
Db6 = Bbm7 = Db6	F#6 = D#m7 = F#6	
Gb6 = Ebm7 = Gb6	C#6 = A#m7 = C#6	
Cb6 = Abm7 = Cb6		

Be sure you understand + can spell, recognize + play in all keys!

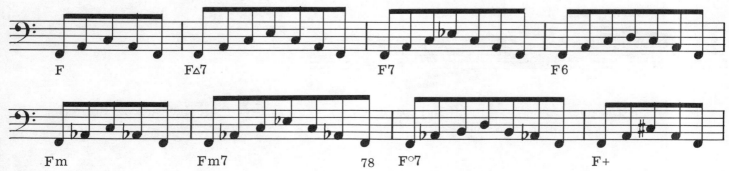

F   F△7   F7   F6

Fm   Fm7   78   F°7   F+

12 M6 Arpeggios in the Cycle

5 Movable Major 6th Arpeggios

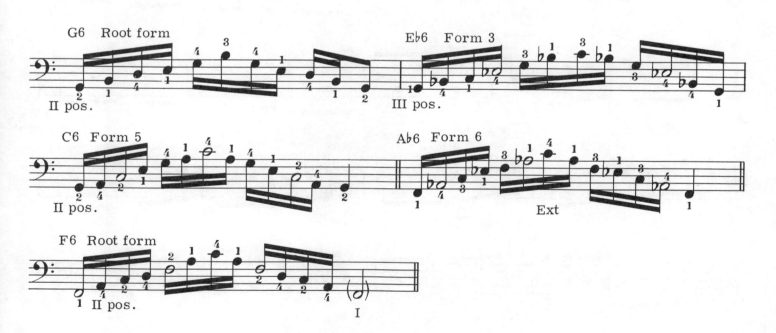

When playing a maj. 6th harmony use the root + 5th as your priority notes.

You can see that although the 2 chords have the same notes the different root and 5th notes outline the different harmonies.

79

III Pos. Etude

The Minor 6th Chord

Construction: ① Play 1 ♭3 5 6 of the major scale.

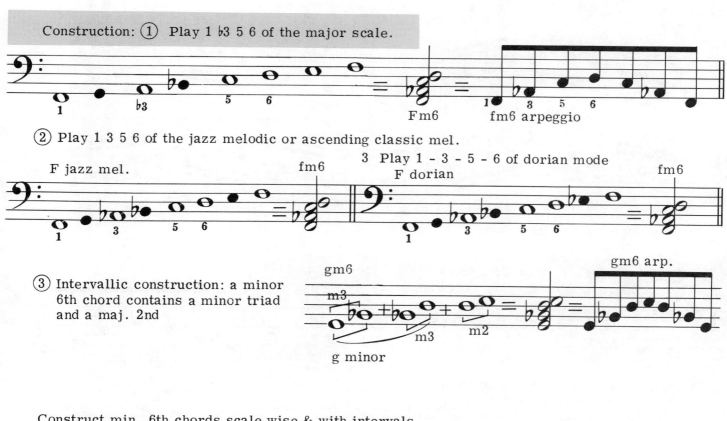

② Play 1 3 5 6 of the jazz melodic or ascending classic mel.

3 Play 1 - 3 - 5 - 6 of dorian mode

③ Intervallic construction: a minor 6th chord contains a minor triad and a maj. 2nd

Construct min. 6th chords scale wise & with intervals

12 minor 6th arpeggios in the cycle

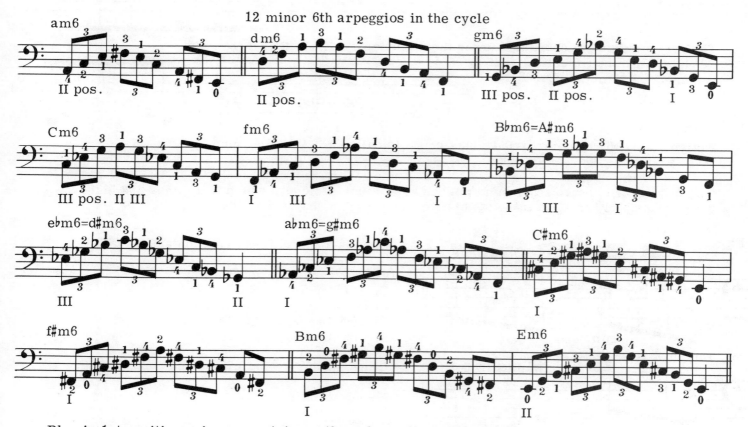

Play in 1st position using open strings, then play pattern fingerings - memorize.

81

4 Movable m6 Arpeggios

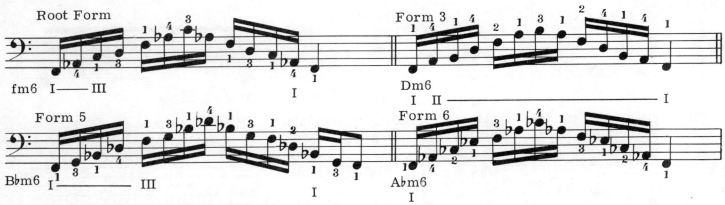

Root Form

fm6 I——III I

Form 3

Dm6 I II ——————————— I

Form 5

Bbm6 I————III I

Form 6

Abm6 I

Play up and down the finger board.

① Minor 7b5 arpeggio or half diminished chord (m7b5)=(m7-5)
Construction: ① Play the 1, b3, b5, b7 notes of the major scale.

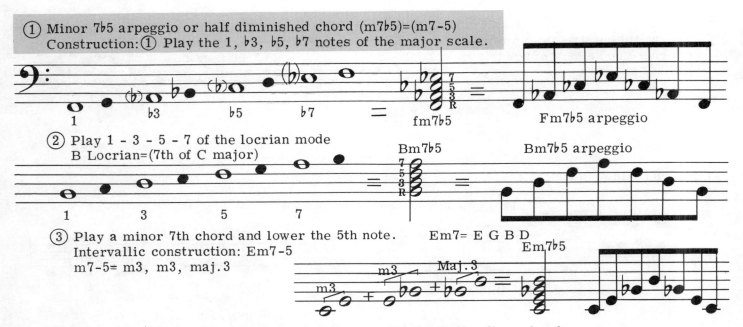

1   b3   b5   b7   fm7b5   Fm7b5 arpeggio

② Play 1 - 3 - 5 - 7 of the locrian mode
B Locrian=(7th of C major)

Bm7b5   Bm7b5 arpeggio

1   3   5   7

③ Play a minor 7th chord and lower the 5th note.   Em7= E G B D
Intervallic construction: Em7-5   Em7b5
m7-5= m3, m3, maj.3

Notice 1, b3, b5, = a dim. triad. This chord is called a half - dim. chord.

The m7b5 chord contains the same pitches as a minor 6th chord which is a minor 3rd higher;
This means a m6 chord has the same notes as a m7b5 a major 6th higher.

Ex

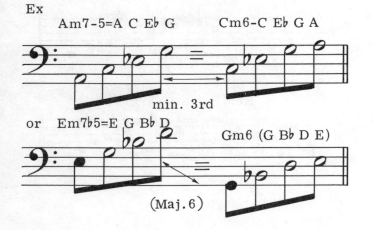

Am7-5=A C Eb G   Cm6-C Eb G A

min. 3rd

or Em7b5=E G Bb D   Gm6 (G Bb D E)

(Maj.6)

Here is a list of these relation ships

gm7b5=Bbm6   em7b5=gm6
Cm7b5=Ebm6   Bm7b5=Dm6
fm7b5=Abm6   F#m7b5=Am6
Bbm7b5=Dbm6   C#m7b5=Em6
Ebm7b5=Gbm6   g#m7b5=Bm6
Abm7b5=Cbm6   d#m7b5=f#m6
G#m7b5=Bm6   a#m7b5=C#m6

Memorize this chart.

The 12 Minor 7♭5 Arpeggios in the I position

4 Movable m7♭5 Forms

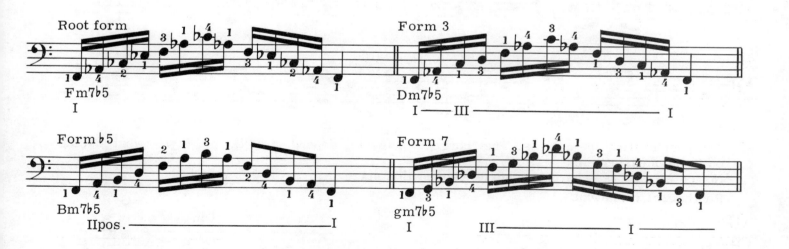

Learn these 4 minor chords thoroughly in all keys

Simple bass lines using chords studied

Progression - Means a group of chords that are related-spell chords before studying or writing exercises.

The possibilities are endless. The "correct" notes are dependent on tempo, style, what's going on in the measure etc.
Notice we only use chordal or scale tones at this stage.
Rhythmical variations-

Invent your own.

Notice on the 1st & 3rd beats we use chordal tones at this stage.

Notice that there isn't too much movement or awkward skips.

After playing - construct some of your own. That's how you learn.

IV + V Position

Drill in IV+V Position Notes

IV+V Position Drill

87

Rhythmical moveable III position pattern scales and arpeggios. The following scales and arpeggios can be played in the III position and should be memorized.

The Dorian Mode

Construction: 1) Play the 2nd note of a major scale to the 2nd note 1 octave higher.

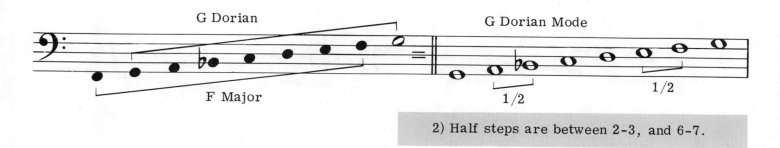

2) Half steps are between 2-3, and 6-7.

3) Play major scale and lower 3 and 7 notes.

4) Play the pure minor scale and raise the 6th note of the scale.

The dorian mode plays through minor harmonies. (m6, m7, m9, m11, and sus. chords)

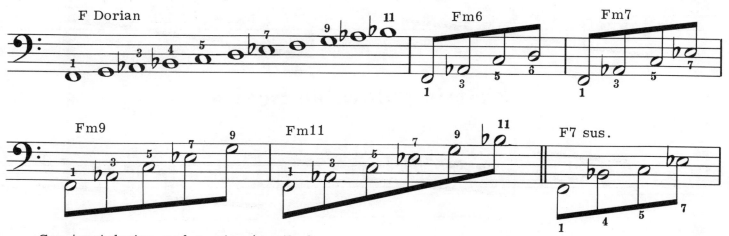

Construct dorian modes using 4 methods.

The 12 dorian modes in the I position

Play ascending and descending

4 String Movable Dorian Scales

3 String Movable Scales

Dorian Patterns

91

Harmonization of the Major Scale

Every bassist must know this thoroughly. Remember the bassist is at the bottom of the harmony which is the most important line along with the melodic construction. If the bass player does not understand what is going on above and cannot hear intervals and harmonies, he is unable to contribute satisfactorily to the group. A "melody" bass player (one who only plays melody notes) is useless. What is needed is the player who hears the "correct or choice" notes and works with the pianist left hand and the harmonic changes that the soloist is trying to build his ideas around. When it is time for a bass solo, then imagination and ideas are called for and the bassist must stress intonation, good sound, and good notes. A good rule to remember is to underplay rather than overplay. This is a definition of good taste, something a musician must develop or he is merely a mechanic.

The G Harmonized Scale in Triads
(3 Part Harmony)

We harmonize the scale by using every other note of the scale.

Every note of the scale is called a degree of the scale.

Starting with the note G write the 3rd note B and the 5th note D . This forms the G chord. Starting next with the 2nd note A, write C and E. Continue this pattern with each note of the scale.

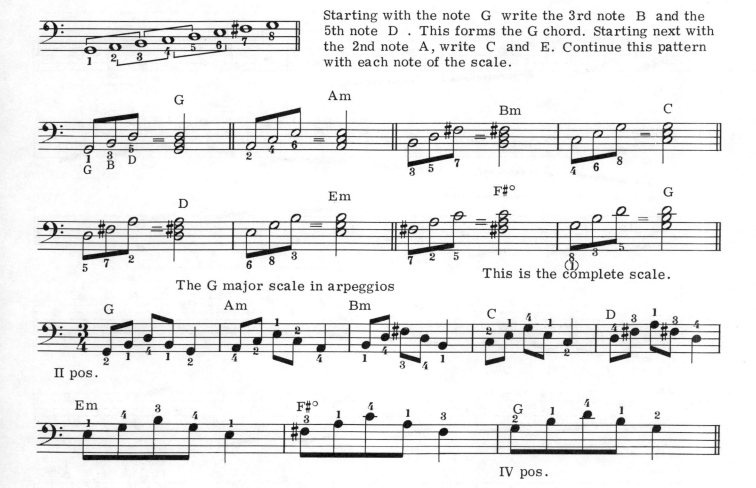

This is the complete scale.

The G major scale in arpeggios

After memorizing the pattern, use the fret guide and play this in all positions.

92

Jazz does not use triadic motion but usually needs 4 note chords to project jazz ideas.

The E major scale harmonized in 4 note chords.

The procedure is the same except we add 1 more note but still use every other note of the scale.

The only change is in the tonic chord pattern which is not movable.

Write the harmonization of all major scales in the cycle of 5ths and then play them as much as possible in the 1st pos.

Key of E major harmonies

This is one of the most important parts of our early training. All players must know the chords in every key and as we become more involved we will learn how they progress - (how they move). This is essentially the basis of all tunes that the bassist will be called on to hear and understand. There are standard progressions that repeat in practically all tunes. By knowing all the harmonies in all keys a major step has been accomplished.

Harmonization of 12 Major Scales in 4 Note Chords

	I Tonic	II Super tonic	Mediant	Sub Dominant	Dominant	Sub mediant	Leading tone
Key C	C△7	Dm7	Em7	F△7	G7	Am7	Bm7b5
F	F△7	gm7	Am7	Bb△7	C7	Dm7	Em7b5
Bb	Bb△7	Cm7	Dm7	Eb△7	F7	gm7	Am7b5
Eb	Eb△7	Fm7	gm7	Ab△7	Bb7	Cm7	Dm7b5
Ab	Ab△7	Bbm7	Cm7	Db△7	Eb7	Fm7	gm7b5
Db	Db△7	Ebm7	Fm7	Gb△7	Ab7	Bbm7	Cm7b5
Gb	Gb△7	Abm7	Bbm7	Cb△7	Db7	Ebm7	Fm7b5
Cb	Cb△7	Dbm7	Ebm7	Fb△7	Gb7	Abm7	Bbm7b5
G	G△7	Am7	Bm7	C△7	D7	Em7	F#m7b5
D	D△7	Em7	F#m7	G△7	A7	Bm7	C#m7b5
A	A△7	Bm7	C#m7	D△7	E7	F#m7	g#m7b5
E	E△7	F#m7	g#m7	A△7	B7	C#m7	D#m7b5
B	B△7	C#m7	D#m7	E△7	F#7	g#m7	A#m7b5
F#	F#△7	g#m7	A#m7	B△7	C#7	D#m7	E#m7b5
C#	C#△7	D#m7	E#m7	F#△7	G#7	A#m7	B#m7b5

Memorize the above table   Teacher and student drill daily

Question	Answer	Spell
Key of F - IV chord	Bb△7	Bb D F A
Key of B - III chord	D#m7	D# F# A# C#

This is what helps to develop the ear, a sound theoretical foundation.

Progressions

A progression is a series of related chords.

Ex. key of C major
$$\left(\begin{matrix} \text{I} & \text{IV} & \text{V} & \text{I} \\ \text{C} & \text{F} & \text{G7} & \text{C} \end{matrix}\right)$$ is the most basic of all progressions

The following is a list of a few bass lines on the I–IV–V–I progressions.

The student is to play the I – IV – V7 – I progressions in arpeggios and then extract lines similar to the 6 examples above in the keys of F, Bb, Eb, Ab, Db, G, D, A, E. (not too fancy)

More Progressions

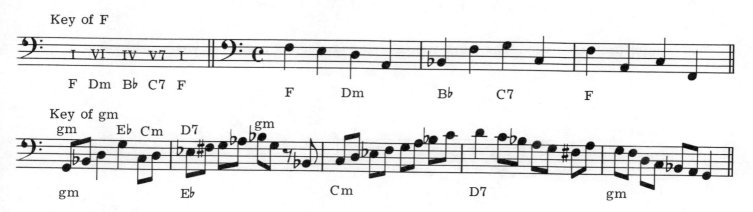

(We will deal in depth with min. harmonizations later)

Key of G:
Bm Em C D7 G
III VI IV V7 I

Key of Fm

III Ab+   VI Db   IV Bbm   V7 C7   I fm

II7 V7 I

This is the most important and common progression in jazz and popular music.

From this point - we will concern ourselves with the altered chords we have studied instead of major and minor sounds.

Key of C - II7   V7   I7
          Dm7 G7 Cmaj.7

Procedure for practicing:
1) Play the arpeggios and scales of the chords in the written progression.
2) Write and play some bass lines using this material.

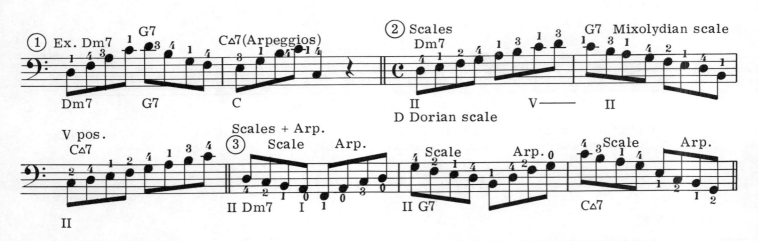

The possibilities are many. The more you experiment, the better player you will become.

Key of F

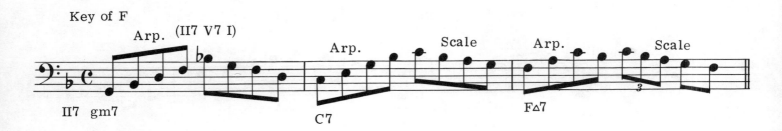

Because of the unfamiliar locrian mode necessary for the m7♭5 and other chords used in minor, we will study this II7♭5, V7, I7 in minor keys later in the book. However, the student must realize that the minor II7 V7 I progressions are important and very common. The (-) refers to minor harmony.

Key of A♭ progression
I△7   III7   VI7   II7   V7   I△6
A♭△7 Cm7   fm7   B♭m7 E♭7 A♭6

1) Student is to play arpeggios and scales before proceeding.

Notice the use of the open string and rest to help change pos. smoothly.

What is important is that: 1) The student can spell and play all the harmonies of the progression by memory.
2) The student practices writing easy passages as above to learn to read more fluently and be able to handle the harmonies with ease in any of the 5 positions learned.

Assignment:
The student is to write progressions of I III VI II V7 I in as many major keys as possible and learn this sequence of harmonies. It appears in thousands of tunes that the bassist will be called on to play and memorize.

97

Chord Movements

Chords basically move by (5th movement — G7 to C,   F7 to B♭
or 4th)   Am to E7 etc.

By step —— C△7 to Dm7   B♭7 to A♭7

By 1/2 step —— C△7 to B7 to B♭7, C#°7 to Dm7

By 3rd or 6th ——⎛Up m3 or Down M6⎞ Up M6 or Down m3
                 ⎝C to E♭m7   ⎠ (C to A7)
                 ⎛C to A♭m7 ⎞ M3   ⎛C to Em7
                 ⎝Down m3   ⎠ or m6   ⎝Up M3, Down m6⎞⎠
                  or Up m6

By tritone   C to F#m7   C to G♭7
A4 or D5   Up A4   Up D5
                  Down D5   Down A4

Write some examples of each kind of movement and play the min. arpeggio form.
Use different keys.

These fundamental movements must be memorized which leads to the important study
of ear training. Throughout the book we have discussed practicing hearing scales,
arpeggios, and chords. At this time the student should incorporate into his studies
at least 1/2 hour of ear training daily.

Ear Training

Student should purchase a tuning fork. Strike the note every 10 minutes until you can
sing the pitch at will.

Interval Recognition

1) Perfect 8 octaves

Do this in the cycle of 5ths

Play   Sing   Then play   Sing   Then play

Use the triad A C# E to help recognize the P. 5ths.
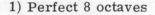
2) Perfect 5ths

Do this in the cycle of 5ths

Play   Sing   Play   Sing   Play

Use the star spangled banner to help.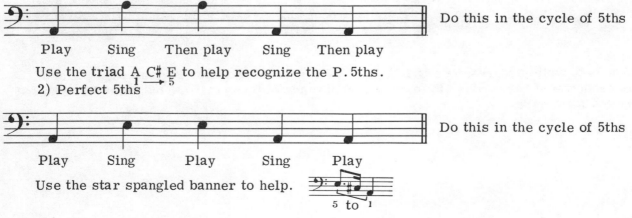
                                         5 to 1

Perfect 4ths

P 4th

P 4th   P 4th

Play   Sing   Play   Sing
                        Check

Use the wedding march

Use chord arpeggio

Look for tunes to help you to hear intervals

Sing P. 4ths and all intervals
following in the cycle of 5ths.

Maj. 2nds

Play   Sing   Play   Sing
                        Check

Use the maj. scale (C D)

Min. 2nds

Play   Sing   Play   Sing
                        Check

7 to 1 in Major scale
B to C

Maj. 3rd

Play   Sing   Play   Sing
                        Check

Use 1st and 3rd of maj. chord

A major

R #3 5

Maj. 3

Min. 3rd

Play   Sing   Play   Sing
                        Check

Use 1st and 3rd of min. chord

A minor

m3

Maj. 6th

Maj. 6

Christmas carol (It came upon the midnight clear)

Play Sing Play Sing
                 Check

Min. 6th

Play   Sing   Play   Sing
                                                Check

2nd inversion of A minor triad

m6

Dm chord
(D F A)

Maj. 7th

Play   Sing   Play   Sing
                        Check

Maj.7

Maj.7

3   5   7

Use the major 7th chord

Min. 7th

Play   Sing   Play   Sing
                        Check

A min. 7th

1   3   5   7

m7   m7

99 Use minor 7th chord

Tritones (D5 or A4)

Use diminished chord

Play D5 / Sing — Play Sing Check — Play A4 / Sing — Play Sing Check — 5th Dim — A4 — D5

After a few weeks, start listening to triadic sounds.

Major chord — Play / Sing Check / Sing Check / Sing Check / Sing Check

Minor chord — Play / Sing / Sing / Sing / Sing Check

1) Along with these triads, sing the major and 4 minor scales.
2) Sing the chromatic scale on the G string.

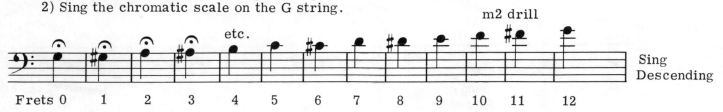

m2 drill

etc.

Sing Descending

Frets 0 1 2 3 4 5 6 7 8 9 10 11 12

3) Now sing the whole tone scale on the G string

Sing Descending

Frets 0 2 4 6 8 10 12

Now that you understand the difficulty in singing whole and half steps, do not spare any pains to become an expert as this can be the most important aspect of your training. If you have an undeveloped or untrained ear, you will always have trouble improvising and playing the correct sound and pitch. Know this - finger technique is not enough. The student should take parts of the ear training exercises and perfect them as he continues with the new material being introduced up the fingerboard. Never let any practice session go by unless you put time in developing your ear. Remember, review is the greatest teacher of all.

1) When you feel you are improving with this work, start singing the dominant 7 arpeggios and dom. 7 scales.
2) Add the whole tone scales and arpeggios.
3) Add the 2 dim. scales and arpeggios.
4) Add the blues scales.
5) Add the major 7th and major 6th arpeggios.
6) Add the minor 7th, minor 7♭5 and minor 6th arpeggios. Space all this work but keep working daily to improve your ear to the fullest.

Major Pentatonic Scales

Construction: 1 2 3 5 6 notes of major scale.

The major pentatonic scale plays through major harmonies and partial minor harmonies, and altered dominant 7th harmonies which will be studied soon.

The 12 Major Pentatonic Scales in the Cycle

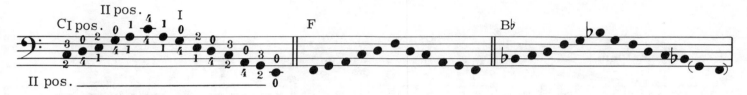

One position pentatonic movable forms

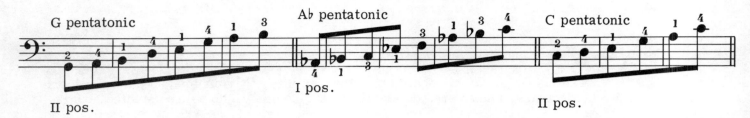

G pentatonic Ab pentatonic C pentatonic

II pos.

I pos.

II pos.

Play ascending and descending

2 position moveable form

G pentatonic

II   IV   II

Play all forms up and down the fingerboard.

2 position moveable form

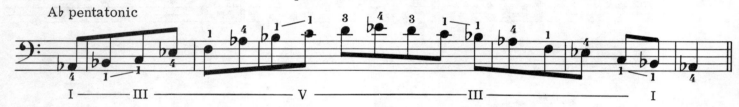

Ab pentatonic

I ———— III ———————————— V ———————— III ———————————— I

2 position moveable form (start on 5th note of the scale)

C pentatonic

II   V   II

one position moveable form (start on 3rd note of the scale)

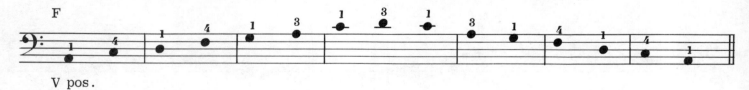

F

V pos.

2 position moveable form (start on 2nd of scale)

II pos. ———————————— IV ———————————— II

102

Major Pentatonic Patterns

The major pentatonic scales generate maj. 6, maj. 9, maj. 6/9, and min. 7, min. 11 and sus. chords. Also notice how many notes of the major pentatonic fit the dom. 7th chord $\frac{1}{2}$ step lower. (c pent. and B7 chord)

103

VI – VII Positions

VI Position Drill

VI Position Note Reading

104

Moveable VII Position Scales and Arpeggios

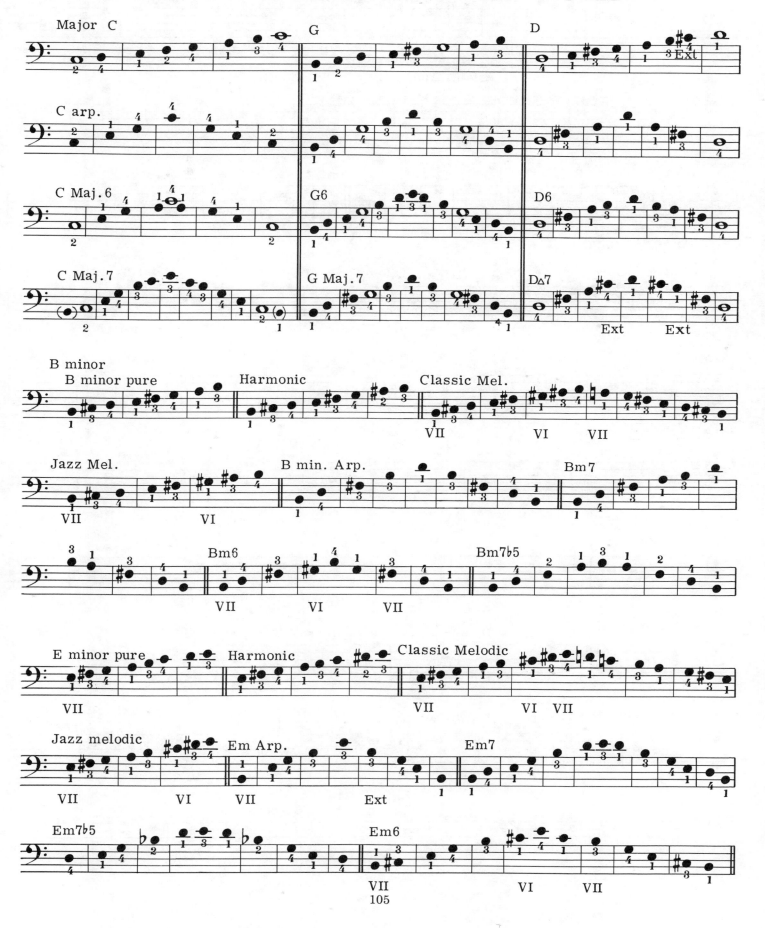

106

Perpetual Motion

The 9th Chords

Construction: Maj. add 9 - play 1 3 5 9 of scale (9 = 2 of scale)

Maj 6/9 = 1 3 5 6 9 of maj. scale

F maj. 6/9

F maj. 9 = 1 3 5 7 9 of scale

F min. add 9 = 1 ♭3 5 9 of the major scale

Fm6/9 = 1 ♭3 5 6 9 of the major scale

F min. 9 = 1 ♭3 5 ♭7 9 of the major scale

Fm7+ (Meaning Fm with a maj. 7th interval instead of the Fm with a min. 7 int.)

F min.9 7+ = 1 ♭3 5 7 9 of maj. scale

F9 = 1 3 5 ♭7 9 of the maj. scale

F7#9 = 1 3 5 ♭7 #9 of the maj. scale

F7♭9 = 1 3 5 ♭7 ♭9 of the maj. scale

F7#9#5 = 1 3 #5 ♭7 #9 of the maj. scale

F7#9 = 1 3 ♭5 ♭7 #9 of the maj. scale
♭5

F7♭9 = 1 3 ♭5 ♭7 ♭9 of the maj. scale
♭5

F7♭9 = 1 3 #5 ♭7 ♭9 of the maj. scale
#5

It is obvious that these are very important jazz chords. To strengthen your ear and increase your knowledge, it is wise to take the time to write out these 9th chords and their arpeggios in the 12 keys and then practice singing the arpeggios and playing them in the 1st position. When you hear the 9th chord with alterations (F7#9♭5) all you do is treat it like a dominant 7th chord and play those dom. 7th pitches and let the soloist and chordal instruments play the altered harmonies. It is well worth repeating that the bassist who can hear these chords and play arpeggios on them will go a long way in playing melodic and interesting choruses when his technique and knowledge of the fingerboard have matured.

Ex. C7#9♭5 Play (Root   ♭5) or   Root,   3rd,   ♭5,   7th
                   (C   G♭)   C   E   G♭ or B♭

Augmented Exercise

I pos.

The Minor Pentatonic Scales

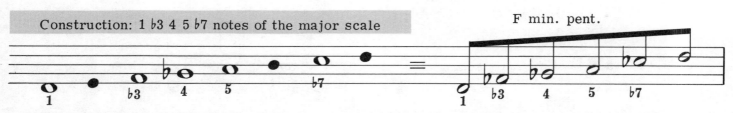

Construction: 1 ♭3 4 5 ♭7 notes of the major scale

F min. pent.

The minor pentatonic scales play through minor harmonies, partial major harmonies and altered dom. chords along with sus. chords.

Ex. C minor pentatonic and a 9th chord (A9 = A C♯ E G B)

C minor pentatonic =	C	E♭	F	G	B♭
The Alt. A 9th chord=	#9	♭5	#5	7	♭9
	B♯		E♯		

The 12 Minor Pentatonic Scales

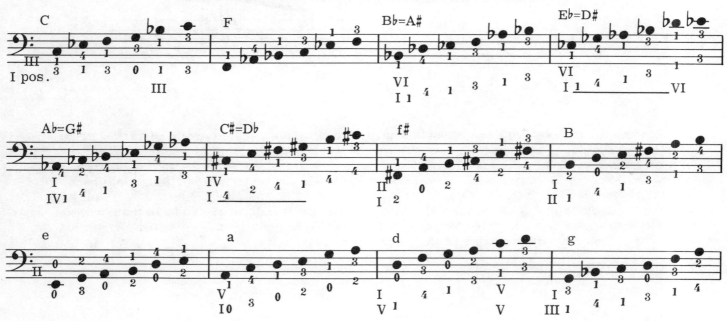

Moveable Pentatonic Minor Scales

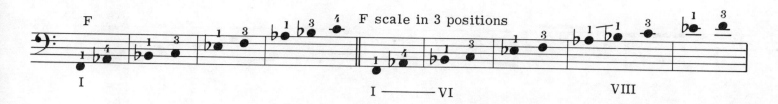

F scale in 3 positions

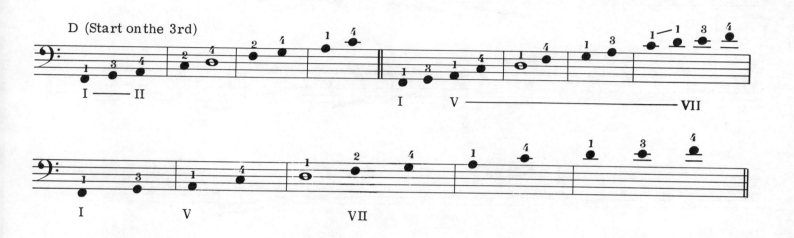

D (Start on the 3rd)

C (Start on the 4th)

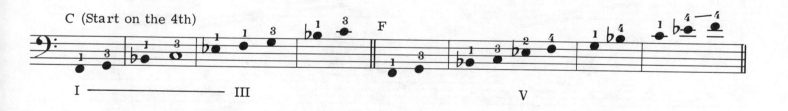

Bb (Start on the 5th)

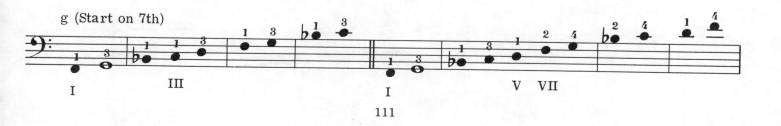

g (Start on 7th)

Minor Pentatonic Patterns

More Altered Dominant 7th Chords

Dom. 7♭5 - construction: 1 3 ♭5 ♭7 of the major scale

② Play 1 3 4 6 of the whole tone scale

Dom. 7♯5 - construction: 1 3 ♯5 ♭7 of the major scale

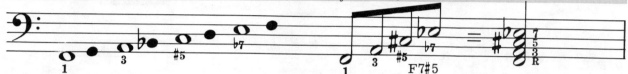

② Play 1 3 5 6 of the whole tone scale

Maj. 7♯5 - construction: 1 3 ♯5 7 of the major scale

Maj. 7♭5 - construction: 1 3 ♭5 7 of the Major scale

Unless the student writes, plays, and listens to these chords, they will always remain strange sounding chords.
1) Construct these chords in the cycle.
2) Play their arpeggios
3) Sing their arpeggios.
4) Listen to them on a keyboard instrument or guitar
5) Memorize their spellings
6) We will deal with these chords in our new scales.

VII Position Etude

114

Harmonization of the Jazz Melodic Scale

Construction: Use every other note of the scale technique.

fm jazz melodic

* Fm7+   Gm7   AbM7#5   Bb7   C7   Dm7b5   Em7b5   This must be memorized

* The Fm7+ chord = minor chord with a major 7th

Arpeggios of the Jazz Melodic Minor Scale

Play this in the 1st position and memorize it.

The F minor jazz melodic arpeggios in moveable patterns.

Memorize and play up and down the fingerboard.

The Phrygian Mode

Construction: 1) Play the 3rd note of the major scale to the 3rd note 1 octave higher.

F major

3rd   phrygian

Notice the key signature of f major and a phrygian are the same.

2) Notice the $\frac{1}{2}$ steps are between the (1-2) and (5-6) notes.

3) Play a pure minor scale with the (♭2nd) note

(new harmony)

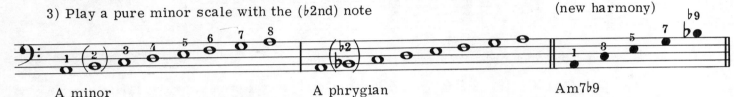

A minor   A phrygian   Am7♭9

The phrygian mode plays through minor harmonies.

The characteristic sound of the phrygian mode is the (♭2) sound.

The new chord is the min. 7th with a flat 9th. (bass plays min. 7th and lets keyboard handle ♭9.)

The 12 phrygian modes in the 1st position

Key signatures will be written to show relationship to major scale.

A or key of F   d or key of B♭   g or key of E♭

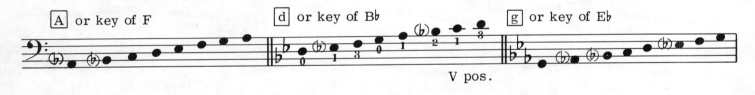

V pos.

C   Ext   f   B♭=A♯

d♯= e♭   g♯=A♭   c♯

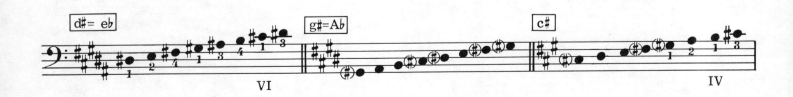

VI   IV

f♯   B   e

Play ascending and descending.   116

Phrygian Moveable Forms

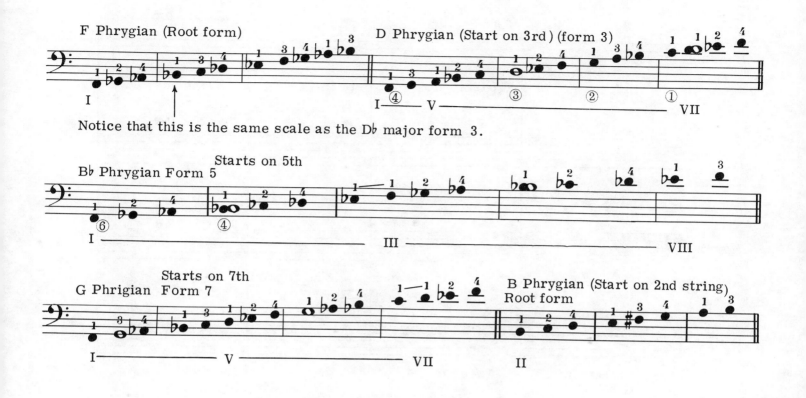

Notice that this is the same scale as the D♭ major form 3.

Phrygian Patterns

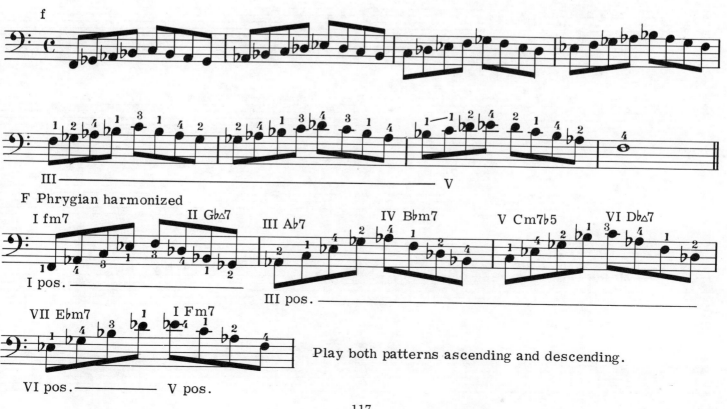

Play both patterns ascending and descending.

X-XIII Frets

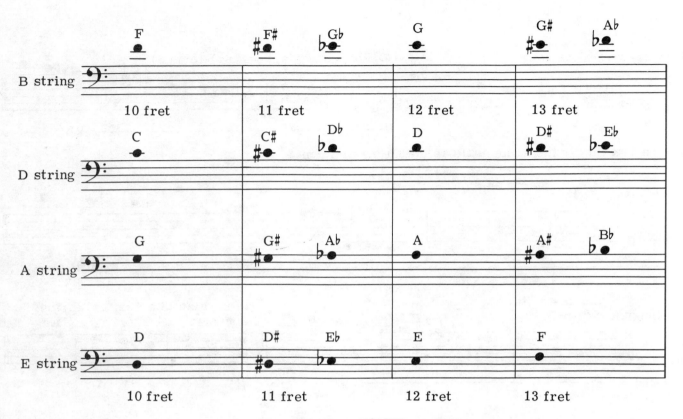

Drill in X Position
(10 - 13 Frets)

118

The 11th, 13th, and Sus. Chords

A dominant 11th chord = 1 3 5 ♭7 9 11 of the major scale.

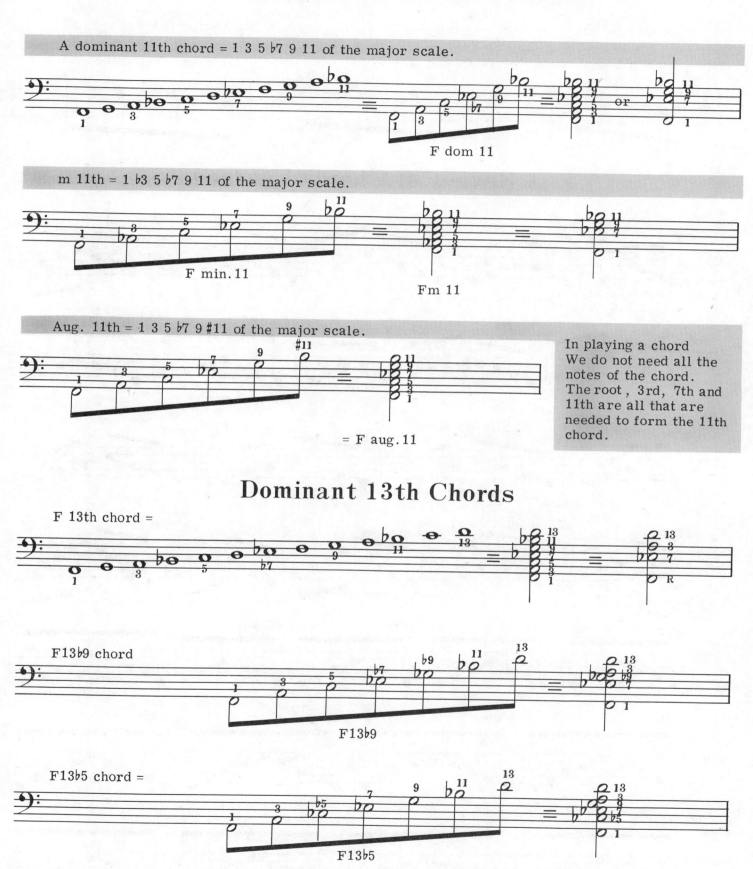

F dom 11

m 11th = 1 ♭3 5 ♭7 9 11 of the major scale.

F min. 11

Fm 11

Aug. 11th = 1 3 5 ♭7 9 #11 of the major scale.

= F aug. 11

In playing a chord
We do not need all the
notes of the chord.
The root , 3rd, 7th and
11th are all that are
needed to form the 11th
chord.

Dominant 13th Chords

F 13th chord =

F13♭9 chord

F13♭9

F13♭5 chord =

F13♭5

Practice playing all these arpeggios in 12 keys.

119

Sus. Chords

By a sus. (suspension) chord, we mean replacing the 3rd of a chord with the 4th of a chord.

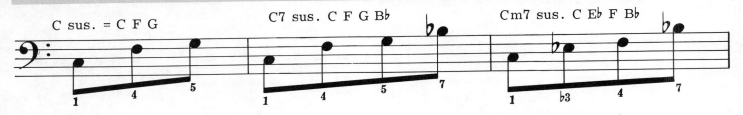

A Review of Chords Learned

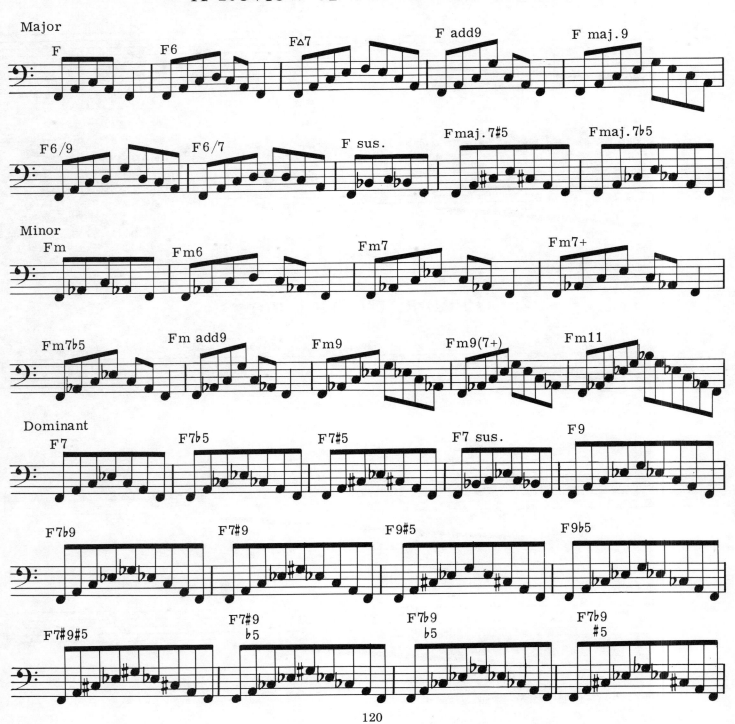

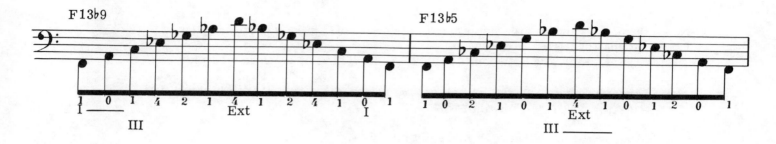

The student should in reviewing these chords understand that there is a great vocabulary of chords which every musician must have memorized and at his fingertips technically. It is important to play these arpeggios in different keys until becoming completely familiar with them.

The 2 Octave Chromatic Scale

Now that we know the 12 frets on each string, we can concentrate on playing all our scales and arpeggios in 2 octave patterns. We must begin thinking laterally, joining positions and extending our ideas and patterns throughout a greater range of the instrument.

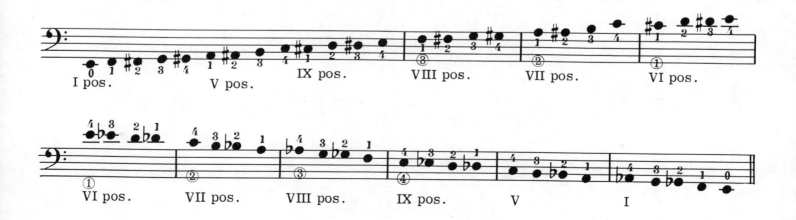

The Lydian Mode

Construction: 1) Play the major scale and raise the 4th degree.

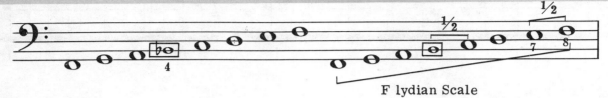

F lydian Scale

2) Notice that it is a C major scale starting on the 4th degree of C major and **extending for** 1 octave to the 4th degree.
3) Notice the $\frac{1}{2}$ steps are between (4-5) and (7-8). Think of your record player.
   45 and 78 R.P.M.
4) Notice that the mode has the key signature of a scale a perfect 4th higher.
   Ex - C major $\left(\begin{matrix} \text{No}\sharp \\ \text{No}\flat \end{matrix}\right)$ - F lydian No$\sharp$ C to F = P4
   No$\flat$

The lydian scale plays through major harmonies.
The characteristic sound of the scale is the #4 note.
The chords that must be learned with this scale are:

F lydian scale -   F maj.7#4 or ♭5;   F maj.9#4 or ♭5   F maj.7#11

We can use both 5th and #4 together.

The 12 Lydian Scales in the 1st Position

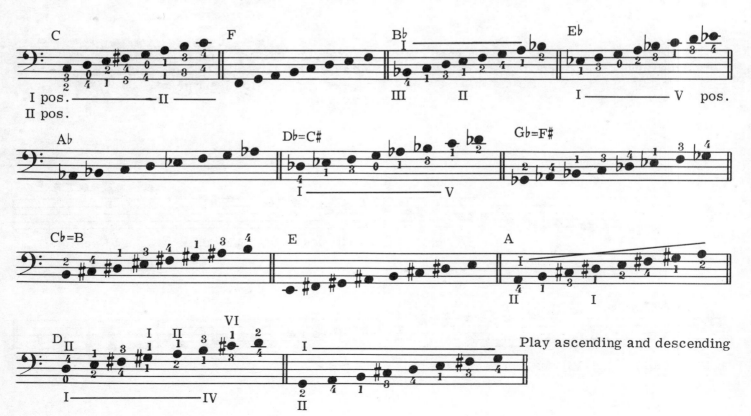

Play ascending and descending

122

The Moveable 2 Octave Lydian Scale

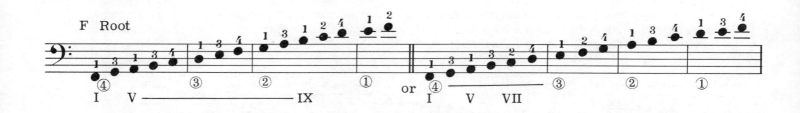

F Root

Db Form 3

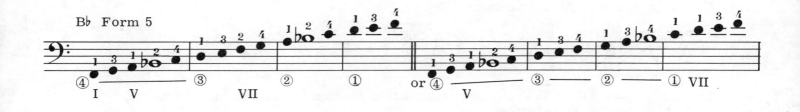

Bb Form 5

Gb Form 7

Root movable G

The Lydian Dominant Scale

Construction: Play the major scale with a #4 and ♭7.

We have learned that the mixolydian scale (also called the dominant scale) is formed by lowering the 7th note of the major scale. By combining the lydian scale (#4) and the dominant scale (♭7) we form the lydian dominant scale.

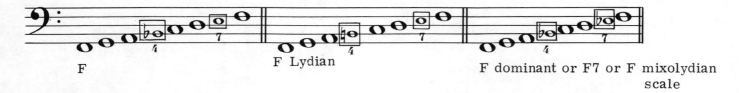

F   F Lydian   F dominant or F7 or F mixolydian
                                                                                    scale

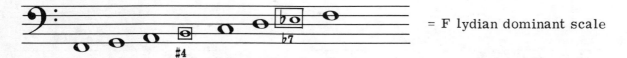

= F lydian dominant scale

This scale plays through the dominant 7♭5 chord.   F7♭5

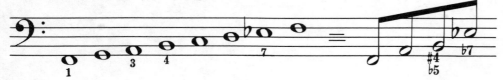

This chord has an enharmonic name: F7♭5 = B7♭5

F7♭5   =   B7♭5   F7-5   C♭E♭
F A(C♭)E♭   B(D#)F A   F A B D# F A
  (B)   (E♭)   B7-5

Anytime we play a dom7♭5 chord, we have another chord a tri-tone distant (A4 or D5) which will have the same pitches.

(C7♭5 = F#7♭5) - (D7♭5 = A♭7♭5) - (A7♭5 = E♭7♭5)
   or G♭7♭5   G#7♭5   D#7♭5

The Lydian Dominant Scales in the 1st Position

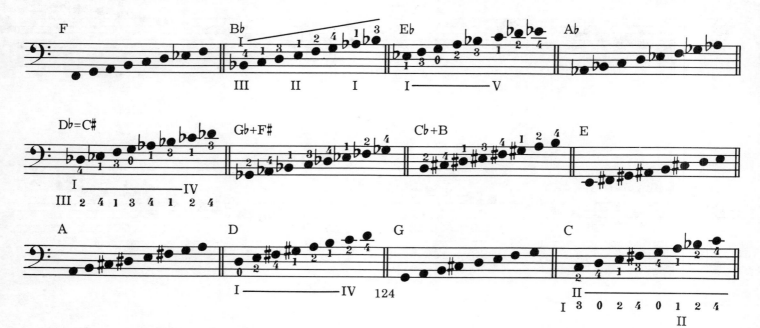

124

The Moveable 2 Octave Lydian Dominant Scales

Moveable Forms in One Position

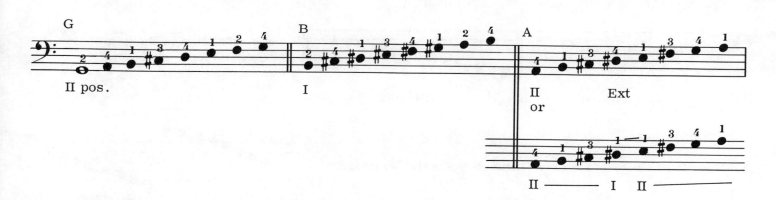

The lydian dominant scale and jazz melodic minor scale are one and the same when related A P5 distant.

C Lyd. Dom.= C D E F# G A Bb C   C to G = P5
G Melodic minor = G A Bb C D E F#

Notice that they both will play through the C7b5 chord.

C Lyd. Dom.   C D E F# G A Bb C   G Mel Min   G A Bb C D E F# G
          R   3 b5   7   7   R   3   b5

             C7b5   E   C7b5
Notice that the Gb Lyd. Dom. = Gb Ab Bb C Db Eb Fb Gb -
                 C7b5 = ⑦ Ⓡ   ③ ⑤
                                  E
Notice that Dbm (P5 higher than Gb Lyd. Dom.) = Db Eb Fb Gb Ab Bb C Db
    (Mel.)
    (Min.)   C7b5 = ③ ⑤   ⑦   R

125

Notice that the G♭ lyd. dom. and the D♭ mel. min. scales have the same pitches because they are a P5 apart.

They are the same and will Play through the same harmonies C7♭5 or G♭7♭5.

$$\left[\binom{\text{G♭}}{\text{Lyd. Dom.}} \text{to} \binom{\text{D♭}}{\text{Mel. Min.}} = \text{P5} \right]$$

Therefore, $\binom{\text{C7♭5}}{\text{G♭7♭5}}$ will be played by 4 scales

C Lyd. Dom. } Tri-tone
G♭ Lyd. Dom. } Apart

G Mel. Minor } Tri-tone
D♭ Mel. minor } Apart

A dominant 7♭5 chord can be played by a scale starting with the same letter, A P5 higher, a tri-tone higher and $\frac{1}{2}$ tone higher.

Play all lyd. dom. scales in the 1st pos. and then play the dom. 7♭5 arpeggio found in the scale and spell it enharmonically.

The Lydian Augmented Scale

Notice that this is the same scale as D mel. min.

The F lyd. aug. scale plays through the maj. 7#5 chord.

D mel. min.   F lyd. aug.

Along with the maj. 7#5 chord, this scale will function beautifully with the (D♭7♭5, D♭7#5, D♭7♭9 and D♭7#9 harmonies)

Now take the tri-tone chord of D♭7♭5 (which is G7♭5) against this scale.

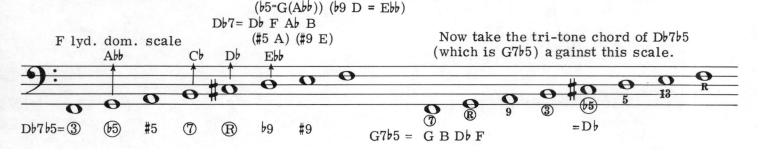

G7♭5 = G B D♭ F

126

What we are trying to learn is that anytime we have a dom. 7♭5 chord, we can always find its enharmonic equivalent in the same function.

The value of this concept is that since a dom. 7th calls for its major and minor tonic, then the 2 dom. 7♭5 chords we find will call for 4 keys. (2 majors and 2 minors)

C7♭5 to F+Fm   You can see that we can think of 4 keys at one time.

G♭7♭5 to C♭+C♭m   Now it becomes obvious that a musician must know theory which always helps the ear to find beautiful and interesting sounds.

The lydian augmented scales in the cycle in the 1st position. Learn pattern forms where written.

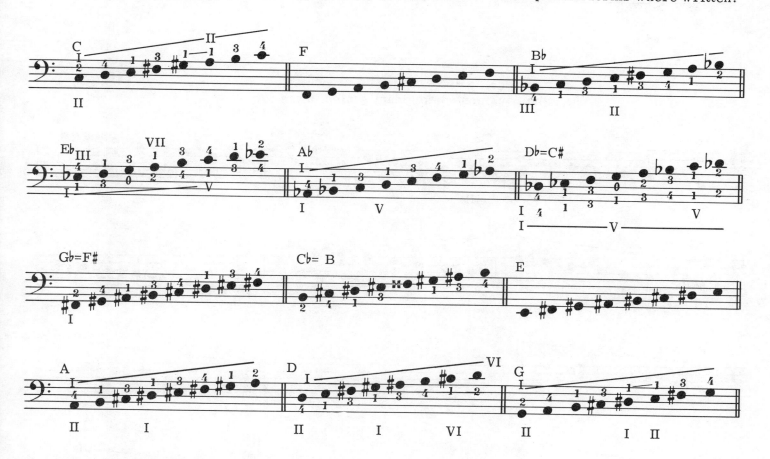

Play ascending and descending

In order to develop more familiarity with the modes, we must spend some time daily working with these sounds. It is advisable to always sing everything you learn both ascending and descending, then make sure you know what you are working with by writing the trilogy of all material in different keys. This is true learning and not the cosmetic knowledge that most students have regarding theory and ear development.

The lydian augmented dominant scale

Construction: Play the major scale and sharp 4 and 5 and flat 7 notes.

F Lyd. Aug. Dom.

This scale plays through the dominant 7♯5 chord.

The lydian augmented dominant scales in the cycle.

This is a difficult scale to sing and should be practiced singing and hearing daily. Do not be discouraged if you can not hear and sing it immediately.

The 2 Octave Moveable Lydian Augmented Scales

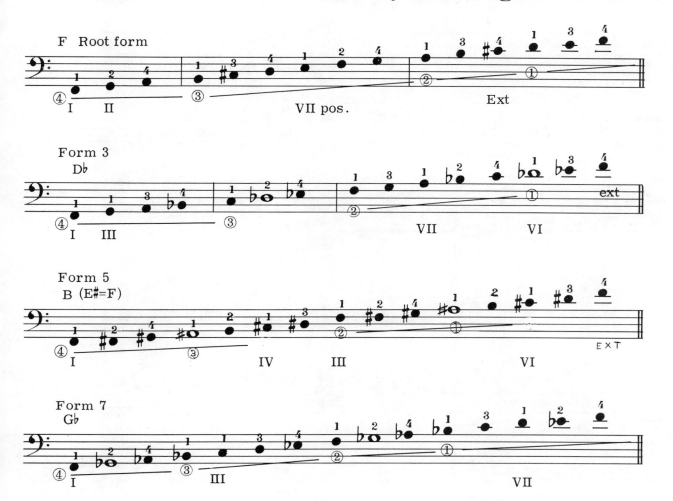

Other Moveable Forms

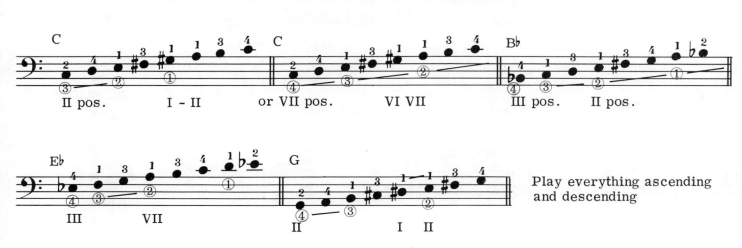

Play everything ascending and descending

The 4 Lydian Type Scale Patterns

32nd Notes

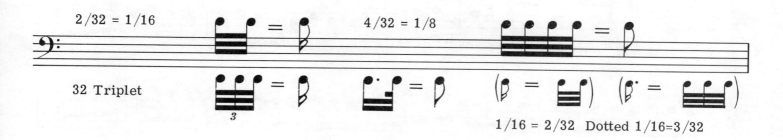

2/32 = 1/16   4/32 = 1/8

32 Triplet

1/16 = 2/32   Dotted 1/16=3/32

etc.

VII pos.   1   +   2   +   3   +   4   +

1   +   2   +   3   +   4   3   +

1/8th Meter

This meter indicates the 1/8 note as the unit of beat.

$\frac{6}{8}$ = 6 beats to measure
    the 1/8 = 1 count

= 1   = 2   = 3   = 4
= 1/2   = 1½   =   (= 1)

$\frac{4}{8}$ = 4 beats to a measure
    the 1/8 = 1 count

= 1   = 2   = 3
= 1/2   = 1/4

= 1/2 a beat

= 1/16 or 1/2 of a beat

Play the above C scale drill in 4/8 time, then in common time until you understand the relative values of the notes.

$\frac{3}{8}$ time = 3 counts to a measure
        1/8 note = 1 count etc.

Tenth Position Drill

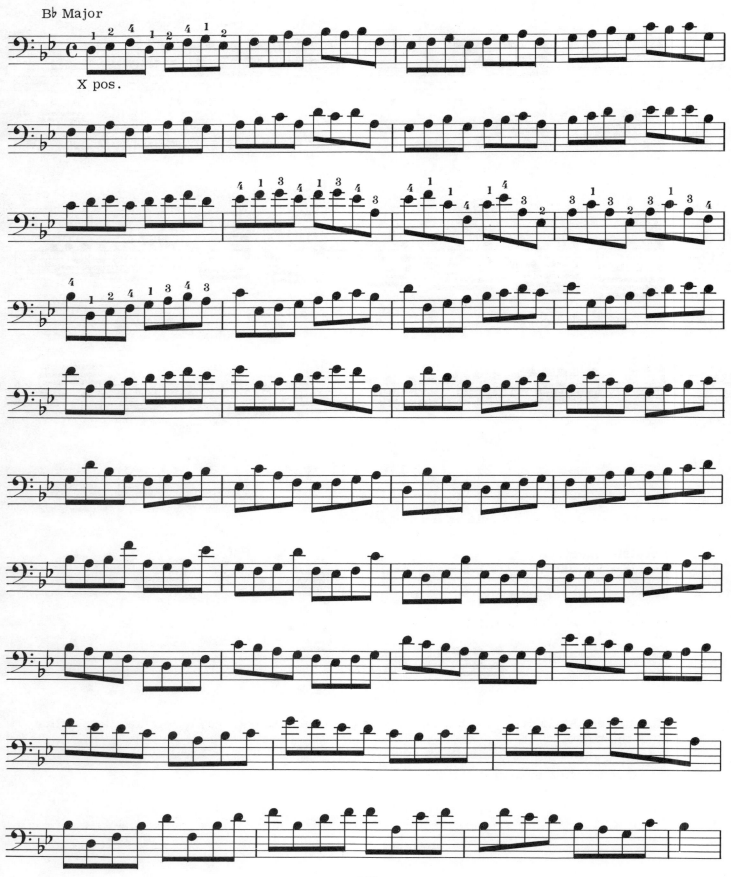

VII and VIII position drill (Aeolian mode = Pure minor scale)

C Minor

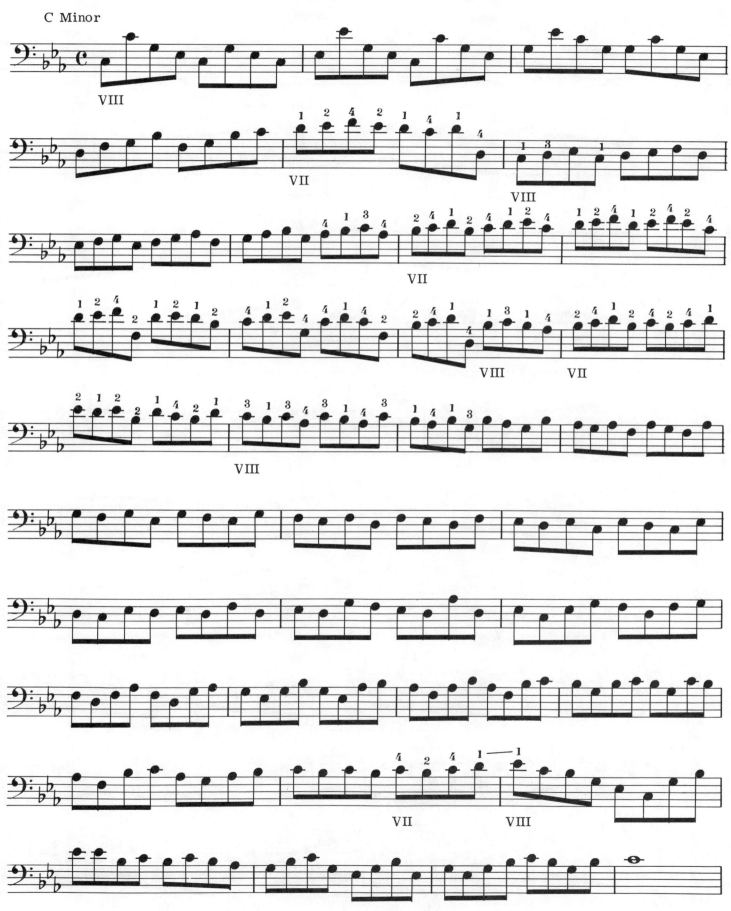

Lydian Arpeggios

The 2 octave arpeggios of major chords and scales

Non-moveable scale C scale

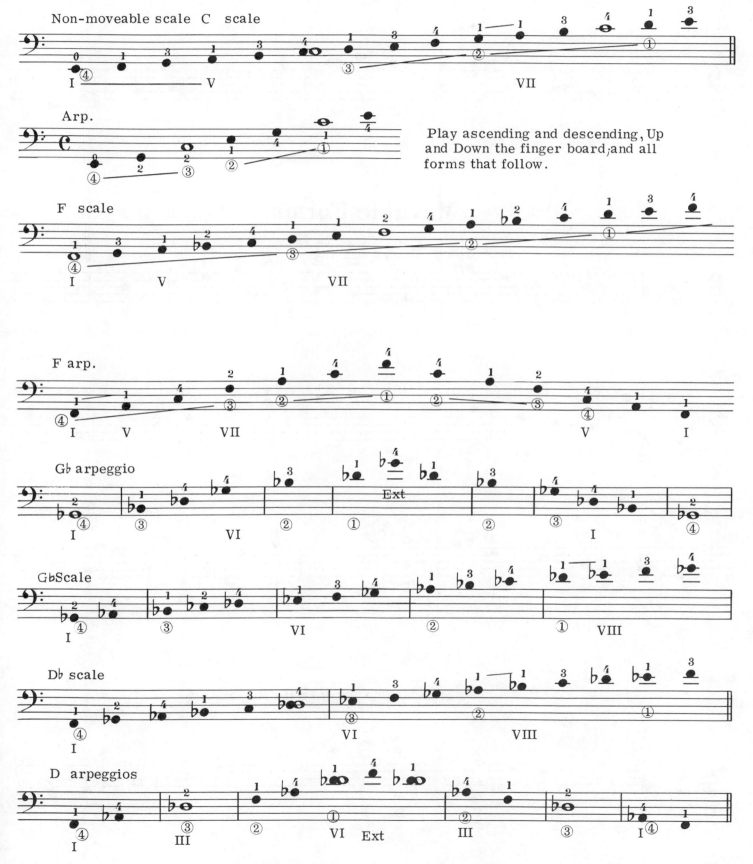

Play ascending and descending, Up and Down the finger board; and all forms that follow.

2 Octave Major 6th Chords

E6

Non movable

Movable Forms

G6

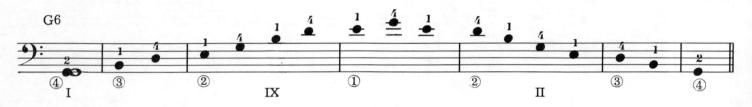

F6   Ext

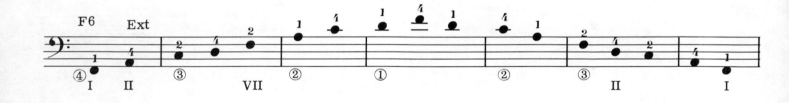

Eb6

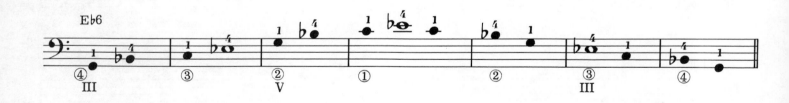

Play all these moveable forms up and down the fingerboard.

C6

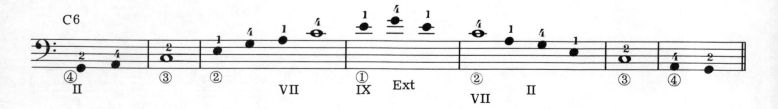

2 Octave Major 7ths

Moveable Forms

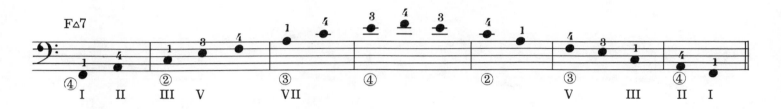

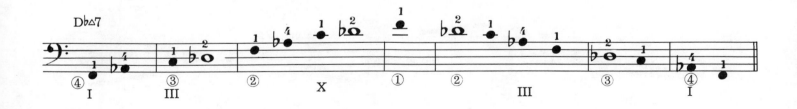

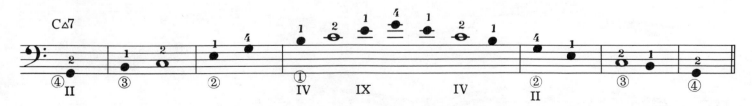

Play all forms throughout the bass.

Harmonization of the Harmonic Minor Scale

Fm Harmonic Minor Scale Arpeggios

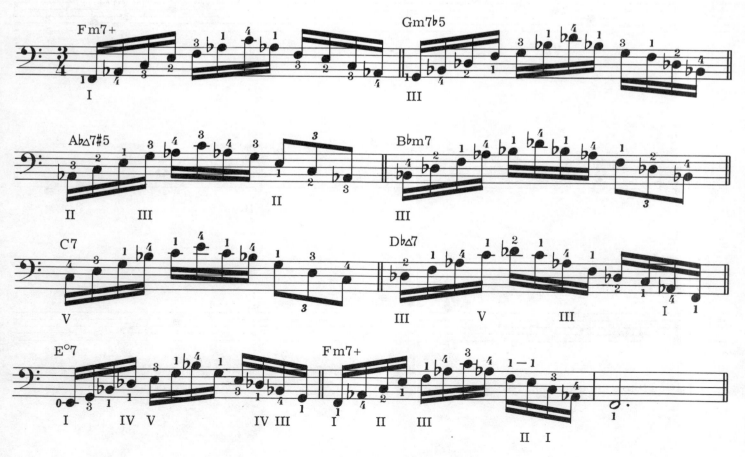

IIm7♭5 V7♭9 I7+

The harmonic minor scale generates the above progression.

139

Review of the Fingerboard

Before progressing above the 12th fret, the student should have a good working knowledge of the following table of notes.

Drill yourself.

Find 5 E's throughout the Guitar

Find 5 C's throughout the Guitar; find B and its octave in 2 places

It should be obvious by now that this **rule** exists: Any note played on a string will be found on a lower pitch string 5 frets higher.

The more you work with this kind of thing, the better reader you will become.

12th Position

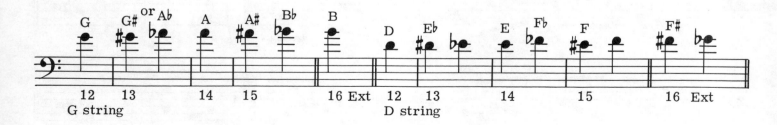

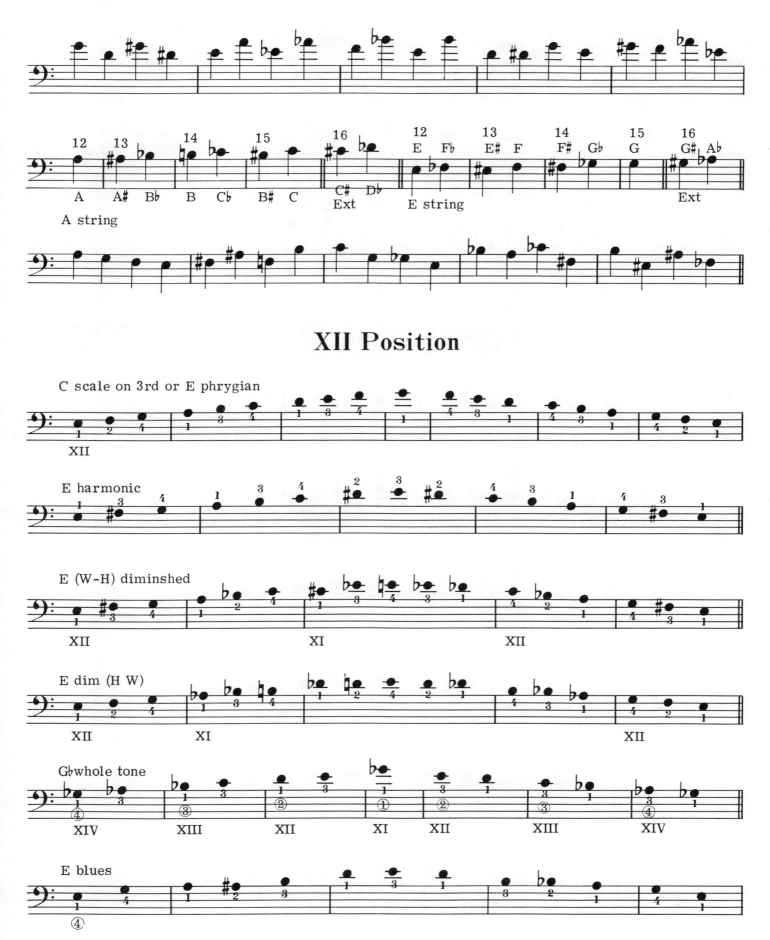

XII Position

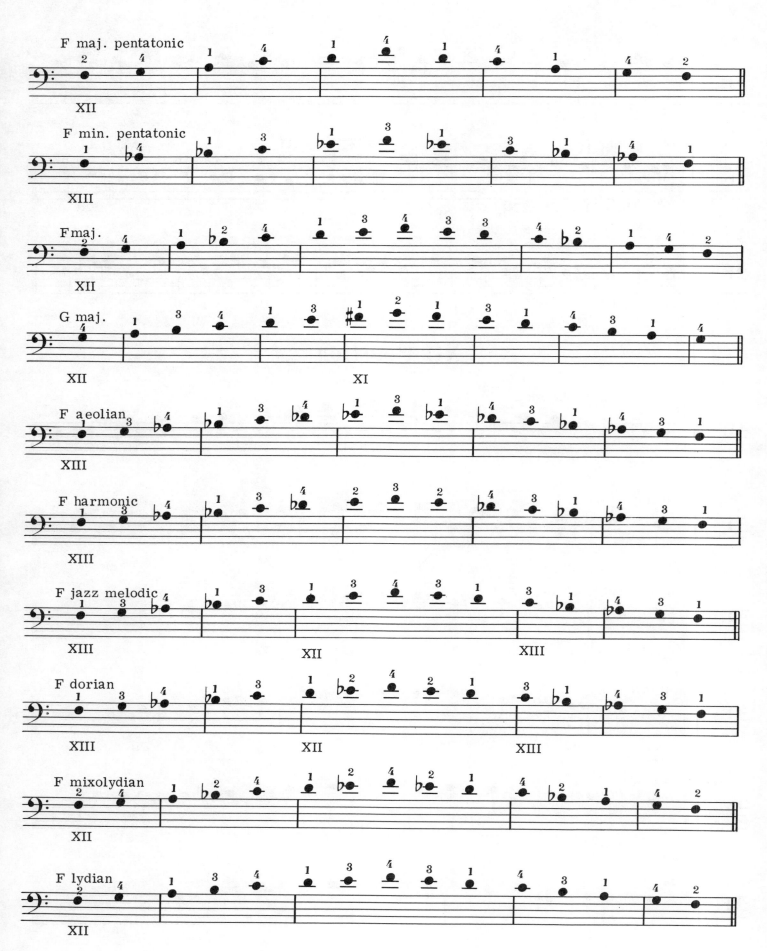

142

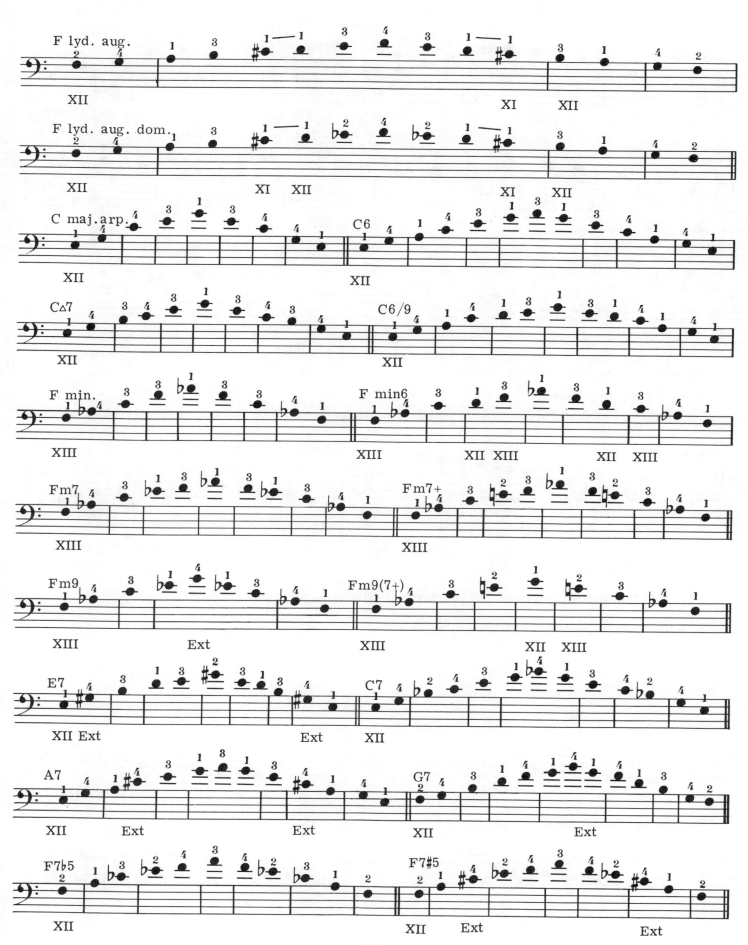

143

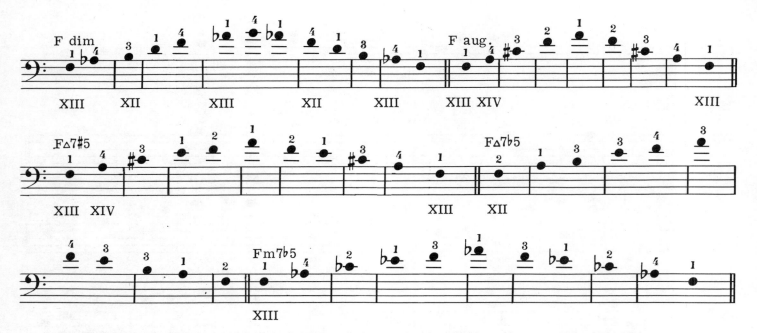

Play these scales and arpeggios until you can become familiar with the higher frets. After playing a while, erase the fingering.

The Locrian Mode

2) Notice that the locrian scale has the same signature as a major scale built on the 2nd degree of the scale.

3) Notice that the half steps are between the (1-2) and (4-5) steps.

4) Build a phrygian scale and lower the 5th note.

The locrian scale plays through the m7♭5 or mø or half diminished chord.

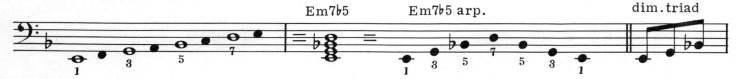

The 12 locrian scales in the cycle in 1st position

The key signature will be written to show the relationship to the major scale.

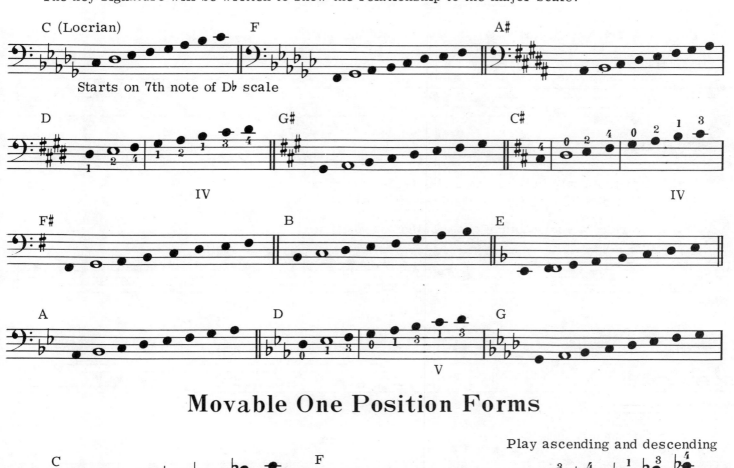

Starts on 7th note of D♭ scale

Movable One Position Forms

Play ascending and descending

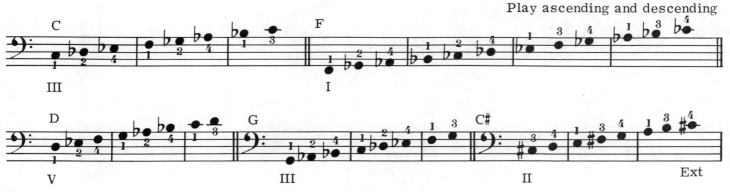

2 Octave Locrian Scales

Play ascending and descending

The Locrian Mode with the ♯2nd Degree

Play the locrian mode and sharp the 2nd note of the scale.

E Locrian

2nd

2

Notice that this scale is the same as the G melodic minor scale.
This scale plays through the Em7♭5 chord. (E G B♭ D)

The 12 locrian #2 scales in the cycle in the 1st position.

One Position Scales

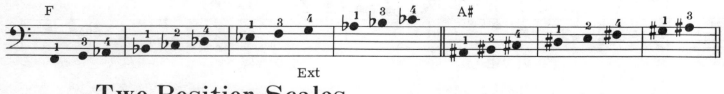

Two Position Scales

2 Octave Locrian ♯2 Scales

Play ascending and descending

The Locrian ♭4 Scale

Play the locrian scale and flat the 4th degree

This scale functions effectively for the altered dominant chords built on the tonic note.
Notice that this scale has the same notes as F jazz melodic minor and the ascending F melodic minor scale.

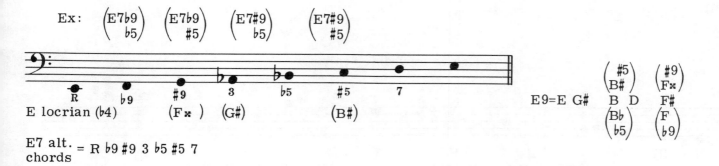

E7 alt.
chords = R ♭9 ♯9 3 ♭5 ♯5 7

In the following scales, write out all altered dominant 7th chords as above in the locrian flat 4 scale example.

The 12 locrian ♭4 scales in the cycle.

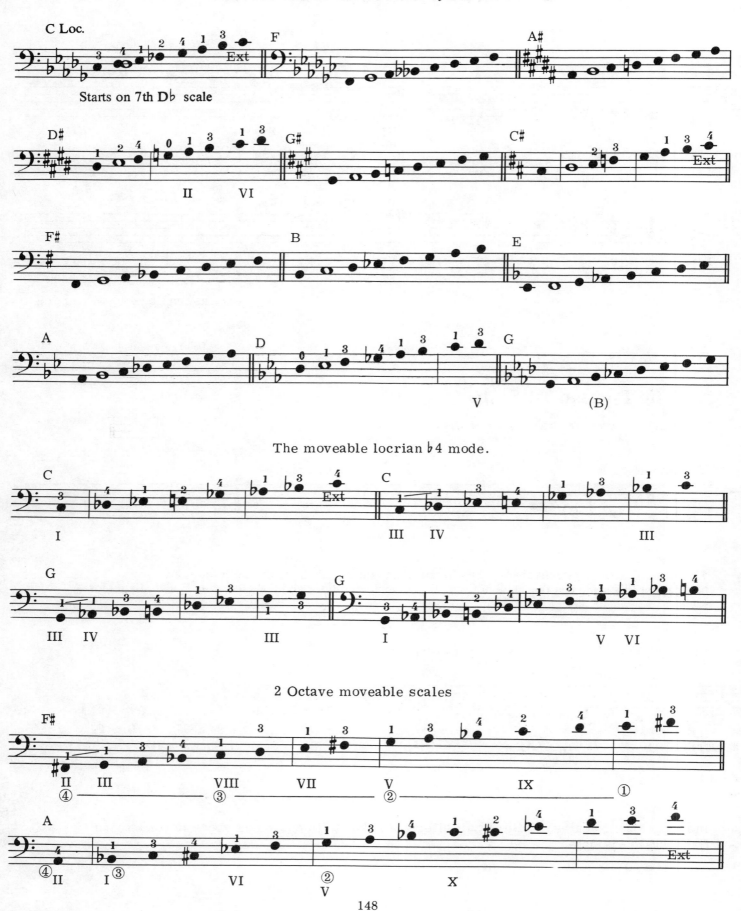

Starts on 7th D♭ scale

The moveable locrian ♭4 mode.

2 Octave moveable scales

148

Locrian ♭4 Altered Dominant moveable Forms

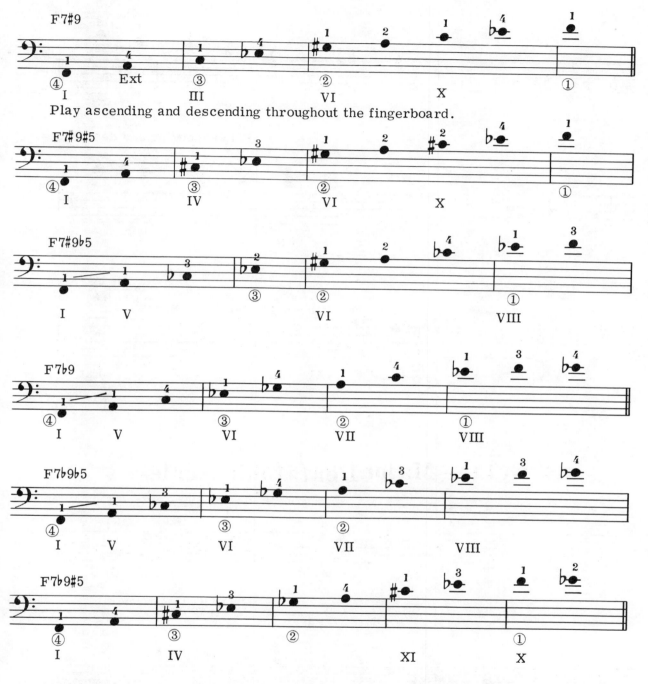

Play ascending and descending throughout the fingerboard.

The author has fingered many scales and arpeggios but the student at this stage of training should begin to use his own fingerings. Many of the moveable patterns have more than one "correct" fingerings and the fingerings written should be used more or less as a guide.

<u>Correct fingering guide:</u> You move smoothly from one sound to another, when you arrive you must be able to move smoothly again regardless of the tempo.

(From somewhere you land, then move again)

2 Octave Blues Scales

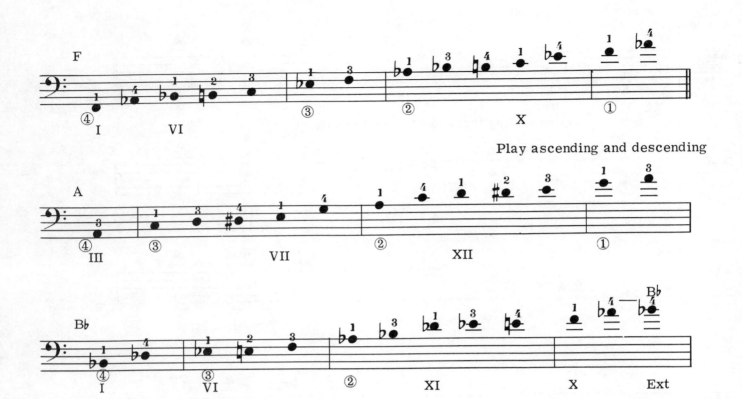

Play ascending and descending

2 Octave Major Pentatonic Scales

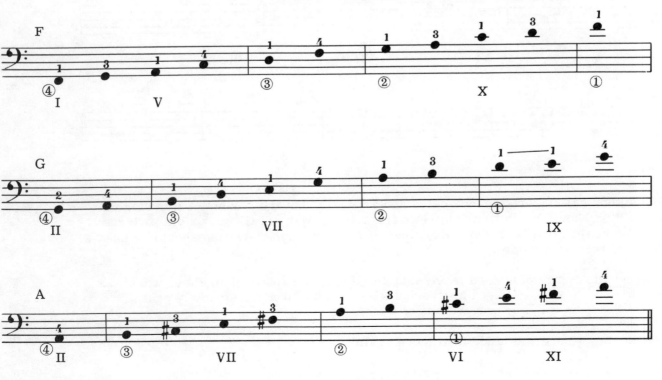

150

2 Octave Minor Pentationic Scales

> Think of a minor 11th chord. (F A♭ C E♭ B♭) these notes form the minor pentationic scale.

Harmonization of the classic melodic minor scale.

The ascending form will be the same as the jazz melodic minor scale.

The descending form becomes the pure form or aeolian mode. It is wise to study and memorize this scale by harmonizing different keys.

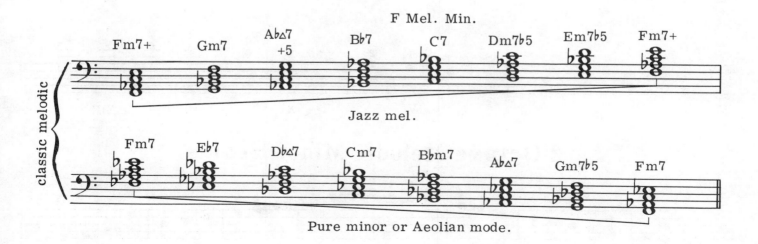

2 Octave Pure Minor Scales

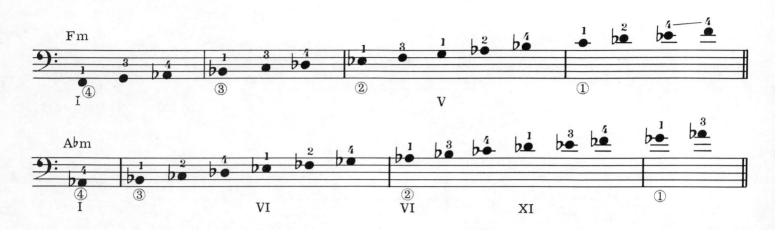

2 Octave Jazz Melodic Mnor Scales

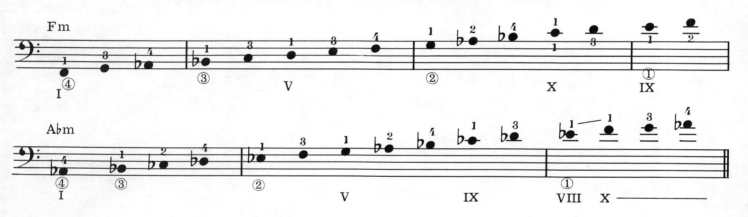

2 Octave Harmonic Minor Scales

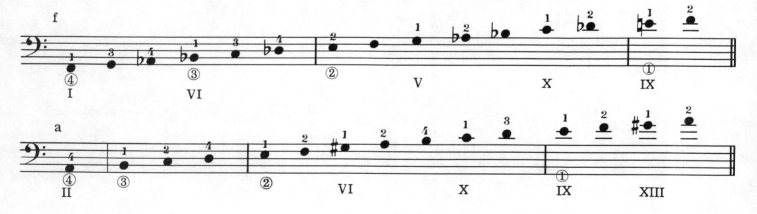

2 Octave Melodic Minor Scales

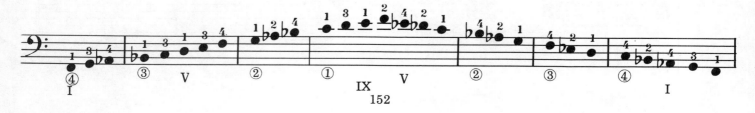

2 Octave Minor Arpeggios

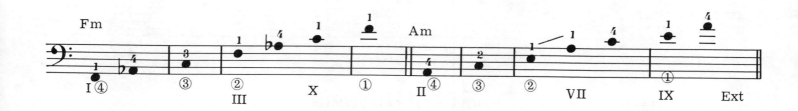

2 Octave Minor 7th Arpeggios

2 Octave Minor 6th Arpeggios

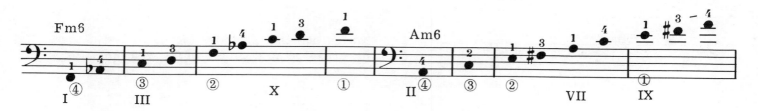

2 Octave Minor 7♭5 Arpeggios

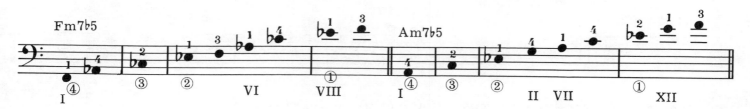

2 Octave Minor 9th Arpeggios

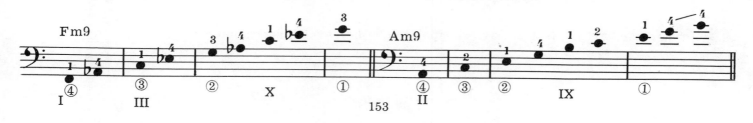

2 Octave Minor 11th Arpeggios

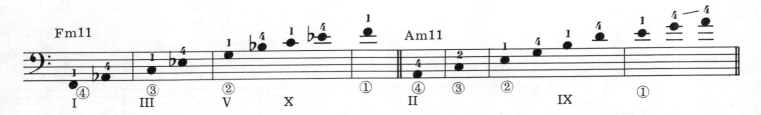

Substitutions

1) The minor 7th chord can and often substitutes a dominant 7th chord. It functions to soften the dominant 7th sound and delays its obvious resolution to the tonic chord.

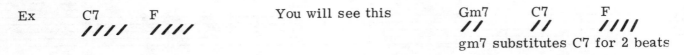

gm7 substitutes C7 for 2 beats

The Gm7 chord is a perfect 5th higher than the C7 chord. (C - G = P5). This gives us a richer and more complete resolution. Notice the fall of the 5th movement in the roots of the chords. This is the most powerful and fundamental root movement in music.

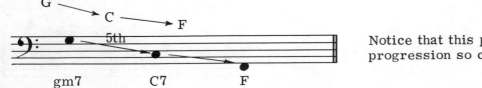

Notice that this provides the II7, V7, I progression so common in pop and jazz.

The student is to practice this progression in all keys by playing V7 to I and then quickly inserting the II7, V7, I sequence. Learn to think fast in any key.

Find your own version - you might want to create a scalewise line.

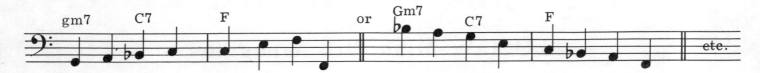

Remember; writing is a valuable weapon to use in learning and memorizing.

154

2) The 2nd substitution that is common is to substitute 2 dom. 7th chords whose roots are a Tri-tone apart. - By using a dominant 7th chord a tri-tone from C7, we get Gb7 or F#7 - C7 to Gb7 = A tri-tone apart. Therefore, Gm7 - Gb7 - FΔ7 may substitute the 1st progression.

3) Another version of the dominant 7b5 is to play the progression.

(Gm7 C7 Fmaj.7)   Play Gm7 C7b5 FΔ7 which is really (gm7 Gb7b5 FΔ7)

C7b5 (C E Gb Bb)
  = Gb7b5 (Gb Bb Dbb Fb)
              C   E

Whenever we have a dominant 7th chord, we can think of the three substitutions outlined.
(Key of G) Ex (I III VI II V7 I)
            (G E7 A7 Dm G7) - (E7 is V7 of A7) (A7 is V7 of Dm)
            Substitution Substitution

4) A dominant 9th chord contains the notes of a minor 6th chord. When we drop the root of the F9th chord, we produce the Cm6 chord.

F9 = F A C Eb G   Cm6 = C Eb G A

(F9 //// |Bb ////) =

Cm6 substitutes F9 for 2 beats.

If we want to stress F harmony, play the root and 5th of the chord instead of root and 5th of the Cm6 chord.

5) Cm6 = Am7b5 - both chords have the same notes
   C Eb G A = A C Eb G - Cm6 (Stress C+G) - (Am7b5 stress A+Eb)
                                              or A +G

Treble Clef

Is the sign for a treble or G clef. It establishes the 2nd line as G. Since parts are written in treble clef, a working knowledge is desirable.

5 Lines   4 Spaces

G Clef Reading Drill

Learn to say these with speed

The Treble Clef Notes Below the Staff

Treble clef pitch
D   C   B   A   G   F   E

Bass clef pitch

D   C   B   A   G   F   E

These notes are on the same strings and frets.

Note Reading Drill in 𝄞

1) First say the notes
2) Play the notes; the trick is to learn to say them with speed.

Guitar

Bass Guitar

Sounds one octave lower.

Transposition

Transposition means to reproduce a musical pitch from one key to another.
Transposition requires a great deal of practice and should be studied seriously.

1) Transposition by letters and frets. (keys of C to F)

1) The rhythm remains the same.

2) Write scales in both keys. Key of C (C D E F G A B C)
Key of F (F G A B♭ C D E F)

3) Both excerpts start with the 1st note of each key.

4) The 2nd note of the key of C is 3 letters and 3 frets lower therefore the 2nd note of the new
key F major must be 3 letters and 3 frets lower. Notice that the 4th note of the 1st measure
is 1 letter and 2 frets lower and when we apply this relationship to the 3rd and 4th letters
in the key of F, we need a B♭ to establish the correct distance of 2 frets.

2) The second method is through intervals.

Key of C – original

Everything in the key of C is a
P5 above the key of F notes.

Key of F New key

1) In the key of C, the 2nd note is a minor 3rd lower from the 1st note. Therefore, the 2nd
note of the key of F must be a minor 3rd lower from the 1st note F, etc.

3) The 3rd method is to think in terms of key signatures and scales.

Key of C $\begin{pmatrix} \text{C D E F G A B C} \\ \text{1 2 3 4 5 6 7 8} \end{pmatrix}$ Key of F $\begin{pmatrix} \text{F G A B♭ C D E F} \\ \text{1 2 3 4 5 6 7 8} \end{pmatrix}$

Just write in the scale numbers.
with key signature

C) Scale notes

4) Transposition of chord charts

The simplest way to do this is to have a complete knowledge of the harmonized scales and know your alphabet and intervals.

Transpose key of F to E♭.

Key of F	F△7	Em7	A9+	D7♭5	Gm7♭5	G♭13	F6/9

We need not concern ourselves with the alterations as they all work the same in each key.

Think: Key of F ⸤F△7 (tonic) - Em7 is 1 letter and 1 fret lower, therefore
New key of E♭ ⸤E♭△7 (tonic)   1 letter lower is D - 1 fret = Dm7 etc.

Key of E♭   ‖   E♭△7 - Dm7 | G9+ C7♭5 ‖

2nd measure - ⎧ A9+ = 5 letters lower or 4 letters higher and is the 3rd of the scale.
⎨ D7♭5 = 5 letters lower and 4 letters higher and is the 6th of the scale, etc.
⎩ or just think everything is 1 letter and 2 frets lower from the key of F to E♭.

2) Use degree steps

F	Em	A	D7	E♭	Dm	G	C7	etc.
I	VII	III	VI	I	VII	III	VI	

158

Chart showing substitution chords

The soloist in playing a chorus continually looks for fresh changes to improvise over. The bass player must help him to seek out these changes and above all, he must hear the substitution chords when they are introduced by the player or the harmonic instruments.

Substitution Exercise

Written harmonies

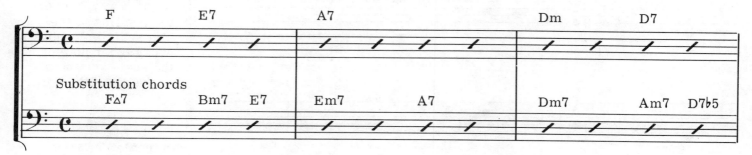

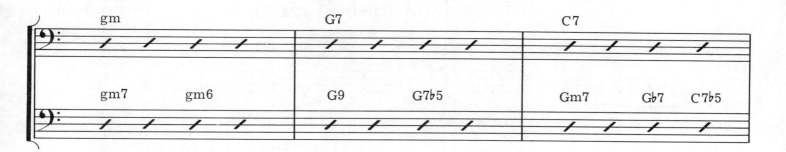

Play the root and 5th notes when you substitute unless you are playing a slow ballad and a rhythmical concept enhances the solo. <u>Don't overplay!</u>

The Whole-Half 2 Octave Dim.Scales

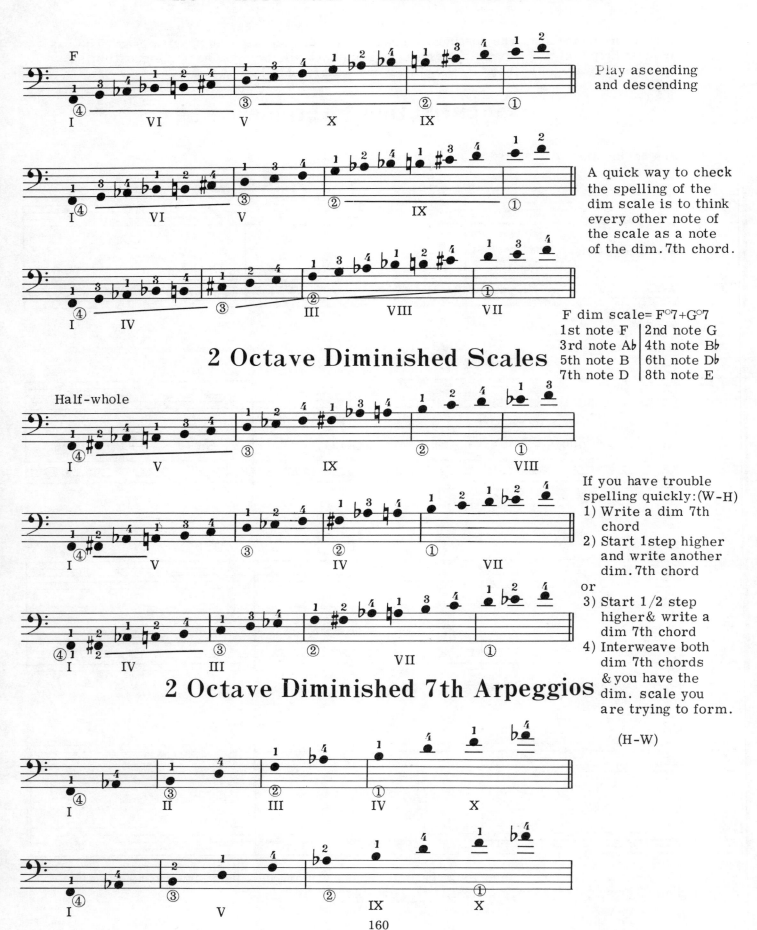

Play ascending
and descending

A quick way to check
the spelling of the
dim scale is to think
every other note of
the scale as a note
of the dim.7th chord.

2 Octave Diminished Scales

F dim scale= F°7+G°7

1st note F	2nd note G
3rd note A♭	4th note B♭
5th note B	6th note D♭
7th note D	8th note E

If you have trouble
spelling quickly:(W-H)
1) Write a dim 7th
   chord
2) Start 1step higher
   and write another
   dim.7th chord
or
3) Start 1/2 step
   higher & write a
   dim 7th chord
4) Interweave both
   dim 7th chords
   & you have the
   dim. scale you
   are trying to form.

(H-W)

2 Octave Diminished 7th Arpeggios

160

2 Octave Whole Tone Scales

Play ascending and descending

2 Octave Whole Tone Arpeggios

Double stops
It is fairly easy to play 2 notes at the same time. These are called double stops.

Use thumb on lowest string

You can do this with any open string as the lowest sound.

Triple Stops Play 3 Strings

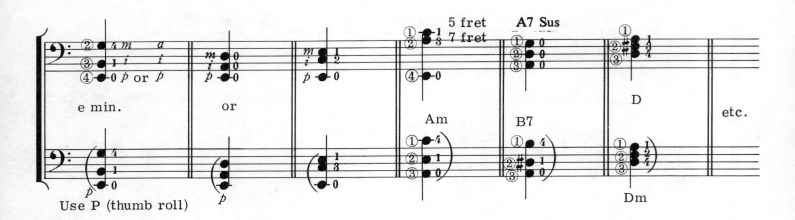

Use P (thumb roll)

Quadruple Stops

The student can see that there are many combinations. Try to find a few combinations using altered sounds.

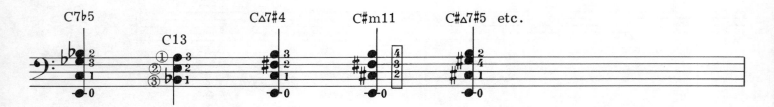

Double Stop Exercise

2 Octave Dorian Scales

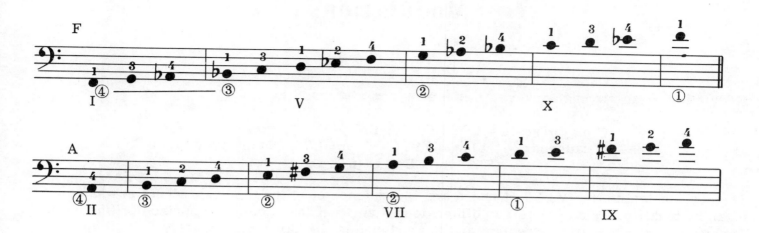

2 Octave Phrygian Scales

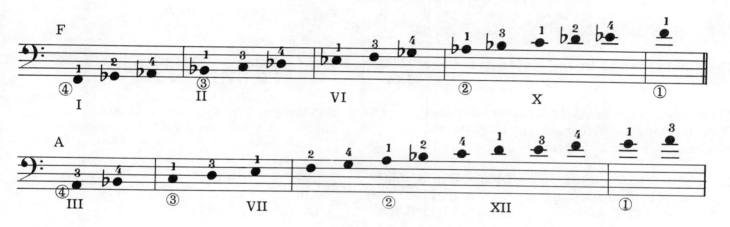

2 Octave Mixolydian Scales

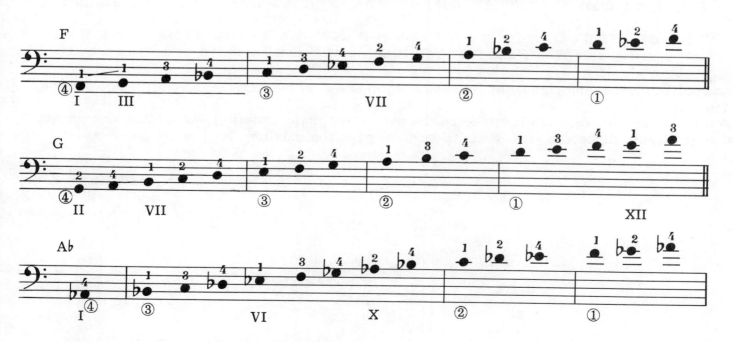

Play all scales ascending and descending.

Modulation

Modulation means to change keys. Key means scale or tonality.

$$\text{C major scale} = (C\ D\ E\ F\ G\ A\ B\ C)$$
$$\text{C cadence} \quad (I) \quad (IV\ V7) \quad (I)\ \text{or(II7 V7 I) or (IV V I)}$$
$$(F\ A\ C)\ (G\ B\ D\ F)\ (C\ E\ G)$$

The scale contains the IV, V7, I chord and the cadence contains the scale. This is what we mean by tonality. Tonality has two dimensions - vertical (harmony) and horizontal (melody). The scale is the melodic ingredient and the cadence is the harmonic aspect.

When we modulate (change keys) we establish a new key center. The II7, V7, I progression is very common in pop and jazz and usually establishes the key or key center.

1) We modulate through the common chord.

The 4 note chords in any major scale are:

Maj	Dom7	Minor	Min7♭5
I,IV7	V7	II7,III7,VI7	VII7

This means that a major chord can appear as I in a certain key and appear as IV or V (3 note chord) in different keys. (V is a 3 note maj. chord but when used as a 4 note chord it becomes a Dom.7 V chord.)

Ex   C△7 = I in C major   Dm7 = II in C maj.   Em7 = III in C maj.
      C△7 =IV in G major   Dm7 = III in B♭ maj.   Em7 = VI in G maj.
  * C = V in F major   Dm7 = VI in F maj.   Em7 = II in D maj.

     F△7 = IV in C maj. * G = V in C maj.   Am7 = VI in C maj.   Bm7♭5 = VII in C maj.
  * F = V in B♭ maj.   G△7 = I in G maj.   Am7 = II in G maj.   But the 3 note Dim.
     F△7 = I in F maj.   G△7 = IV in D maj.   Am7 = III in F maj. chord appears in 3 keys.
                                                     (not used here)

  * C is the I of C, IV G, and V of F but when it is used as a maj.7th (4 note chord), it can only function as a I7 of F and IV7 of G. It becomes a dom 7th chord as a V7 in the key of F.

The student must memorize or at least be able to name with speed these relationships in the major keys.

Remember; theoretical knowledge helps the ear to find many beautiful and interesting sounds. Other professional people know their theory, why not the musician?

Most pieces of substantial length will modulate during the course of the composition. However, some pieces do not modulate but "invade" another tonality only to immediately come back to the original key.

Problem - Modulate from the key of F major to G major by the common chord method.

Step #1 - Write the chords in the key of F. (F gm Am B♭ C Dm E°)
or F△7 gm7 Am7 B♭△7 C7 Dm7 Em7♭5
                          V7

Step #2 - Ask yourself what are the chords in the key of G.
G Am Bm C D Em F♯°
or G△7 Am7 Bm7 C△7 D7 Em7 F♯m7♭5

What are the common chords of both keys?

Am7 = Key of F III   {Am7}
Am7 = Key of G II   {Am } are common to both keys

Step #3 - Write a cadence (I IV V7 I) in the key of F and then write the modulating or pivot chord (Am7), then write a cadence in the key of G major using the (I IV V7 I) chords of G major.

Step #4   F△7 B♭△7 C7 F△7 | Key of F III7 | G△7 C△7 D7 G△7
                                     | Am7 |
           Key of F | Cadence | | Key of GII7 | | Cadence | in key of G

Step #5 - Now play the arpeggios of the chords in this progression.

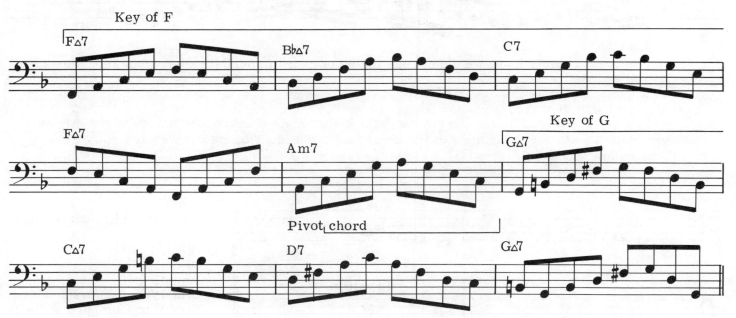

We could have used the {Am chord
                  or {C chord if we had intended working with 3 note chords.

2) Modulate through a change of mode. (major to minor)

The major scale and tonic harmonic minor scale have the same dom. 7th chord and this allows for a common chord.

F major V7=C7   F Har. minor V7=C7
Modulate from E major to E minor   (B7 is V7 of E + Em)

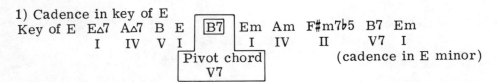

1) Cadence in key of E
Key of E E△7 A△7 B E   B7   Em Am F#m7♭5 B7 Em
          I   IV   V I   I   IV   II   V7 I
                         Pivot chord   (cadence in E minor)
                         V7

We can use arpeggios or scales to play the modulation

Notice in our 2 modulations, we did not use the pivot chord in our 1st cadence but kept it as a surprise weapon.

3) Modulate with the minor sub-dominant.
This simply means to lower the 6th note of a major scale $\frac{1}{2}$ step which now forms a minor chord on the 4th degree instead of the usual major chord. This means we have more keys with common chords.

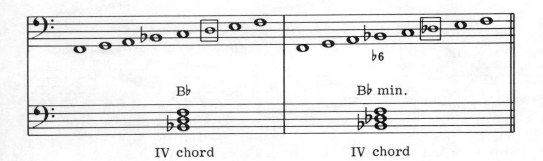

Keys with B♭ minor triad.

B♭m=I in B♭m
B♭m=II in A♭
B♭m=III in G♭
B♭m=IV in F-min sub dom
B♭m=V in E♭m pure scale
B♭m=VI in D♭

166

You will notice that we can modulate with triads or 4 note chords. Using 4 nnd 5 note chords sounds more modern and allows us to capture the jazz flavor. However, in our early stages of modulation which we are discussing in this book, we will use both triads and 4 or 5 note chords.

Modulate with the minor sub-dominant from the key of F to the key of A♭.

1) Cadence in F

F△7	gm7	C7	F△7	B♭m7			Key of A♭				
I	II	V7	I	m IV7 in key of F	Cm7	Fm7	D♭△	B♭m7	E♭7	A♭△7
F maj. cadence				m II7 in key of A♭	III	VI	IV	II	V7	I

Again play arpeggios or scales through the progression.

4) Modulation with diminished 7th chords.

Dim. 7th chords have enharmonic spellings and therefore the same Dim. 7th chord can be found in more than one key.

B°7 = B D F A♭   Which is = To   G# B D F   Which is = To   D F A♭ C♭

Which is = to F A♭ B D   (G#°7)   (D°7)

     (F°7)

C D E F G A♭ B C

B°7 = VII chord in C major (using min. sub. dom. scale) and C har. min. scale
G#°7 = VII chord in A major (using min. sub. dom. scale) and A har. min. scale
D°7 = VII chord in E♭ major (using min. sub. dom. scale) and E♭ har. min. scale
F°7 = VII chord in (G♭ major) (using min. sub. dom. scale) and G♭ har. min. scale
                (F# major)   F# har. min. scale

We now can modulate to every one of these keys with this highly modulatory chord.

Modulate from the key of C to the key of E♭ (We can use different added C scale notes to the C and F chords and any altered dom. 7th)

Cadence in C

I	IV	V7	I	Pivot Chord		Key of E♭				
C△7	F△7	G7	C△7	B°7 (CVII)						
C6	F△6	G9		= D°7 (E♭ VII)	gm7	Cm7	Fm7	B♭7	E♭△7
C6/9	F6/9	G11			III	VI	II	V7	I
C△9		G13							
		G7♭9 etc.							
all C	all F	G7♭5							
		all G7							

. Play arpeggios or scales

all these chords are correct.

The few modulations we have discussed should show the students the importance of knowing all the chords found on every degree of the scale. Each modulation should be memorized and if possible played as harmonies on keyboard instruments or guitar. The student must practice each modulation in a variety of keys especially keys which are not played every day. There are more ways to modulate but in essence they use the different ideas expressed in the 4 different types of modulation discussed. Remember to effect a modulation, play (II V7 I) in the new key and no matter how crude your technique, you will have established the new key center. It is important to know that a change of key has taken place even if you can not hear all the changes. Look for the II7 V7 I.

Ex. Key of C - | Em7   Am7 | Dm7   G7   C△7 ‖ F#m7   Em7 | Ebm7   Ab13 | Db△7

Key of C

II7   V7   I

Key of Db

Turnarounds

A turnaround is a progression of chords that is written at the end of a phrase for usually two measures that substitutes for the I chord and leads back to the beginning phrase. There are many possibilities but we will discuss a few of the common progressions used. As always, the inventive and well prepared student is the one who prospers the most from this type of technique.

You should notice that the turnarounds have ended with some sort of dominant sound which would lead the harmony back to the I or tonic chord.

In the following progression

Key of F ‖ G7   C7 | F△7 | F△7 | use
Bar 1 | Bar 2 | Bar3
(or C7)

Any of these 11 turnarounds (and there are many more) will lead you back to the I chord as they all end on a dominant function.

	F△7 Bar 2		F△7 or C7 Bar 3	
1)	Am7	Dm7	gm7	C7
2)	Am7	D7	gm7b5	C13
3)	A7b5	D7	gm9	C7b9
4)	F△7	Ab7	Db11	Gb13
5)	F△7	Abm7	Dbm7	C7#9
6)	Am11	Dm7b5	Gm9	C7b5
7)	A13b9	D7b5	Gb7	C7b9
8)	Ebm7	Dm7	Db7	C7b5
9)	Eb7	Abm7	Gm7	Gb7b5
10)	F△7	F#°7	gm9	C7b5
11)	F△7	Ebm7	Abm7	Gm7 Gb7

In the following turnarounds, we will write progressions which will lead back to the II7, V7, I cadence either in major or minor keys. The chords used can be either major, minor, or dominant depending how they are used. The student should always experiment and probe to find combinations of sounds he enjoys and certainly must recognize the harmonies if he is to play effectively with good players.

In the following progression use the list of turn arounds.

		Bar 2	Bar 3		Bar 2		Bar 3	
Key of F ‖	A7♭5	Dm7	G7 C7	1) F△7	gm7	Am7	D7
				2) F△7	g7-5	A7	Dm7
				3) F△7	D7	A7♭5	A♭m7
				4) F△7	Em7	E♭m7	Dm7
These 11 turnarounds will lead back to the II chord (Gm7) (Gm9) etc + then to the V7 I chord. There are many more.				5) F△7	E♭7	A9	A♭m7
				6) F△7	E7	Am11	D7♭5
				7) F△7	Gm7	Am7	A♭m7
				8) Am7	D7	A♭7	D♭7
				9) F△7	Em7	A7♭5	Gm7
				10) F△7	B♭△7	Am7	A♭m7
				11) F△7	F♯o7	Gm7	A♭m7

Turnaround #1 leading to tonic

Turnaround #2 leading to dominant

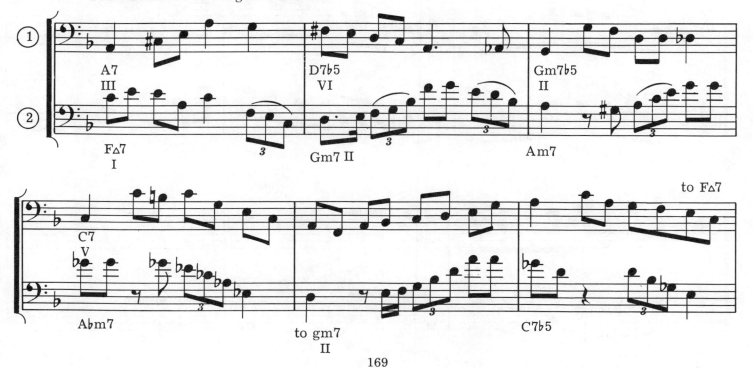

Every musician should learn to play duets as they probably require the most training and skill. Play both parts of the following duet with another bass or guitar or pianist. Listen to the other part while you play and surrender to his phrasing to develop a tight sound, then reverse this idea.

Duet in Early Bop Style

Moving tempo

Bass I

Bass II

Chord Movements and their Relative Functions

We have learned that the tonic major 7th chord usually establishes a tonal center if not a tonality and that the dominant 7th looks for its tonic chord. But, we must observe some functional movement by other degree harmonies in the scale.

The II chord (m7 or Dom 7) usually moves to the V degree as in our II7, V7, I or (IIm7b5, Vb9, Im7) or it along with the bII can move down a $\frac{1}{2}$ step and a 5th.

Ex. $\left(\begin{array}{cc} Dm7 & G7 \quad C \\ \searrow 5th \end{array}\right)$ $\left(\begin{array}{cc} Dm7 & Db7 \quad C \\ \searrow 1/2\ step \end{array}\right)$ $\left(\begin{array}{cc} Dm7 & Db7 \quad C \\ \searrow 1/2\ step \end{array}\right)$

II7   II7   II7

The bII7 will sound effective in the progression. $\left(\begin{array}{cccc} II7 & bII7 & bVM7 & IM7 \\ Dm7 & Db7 & GbM7 & C\triangle7 \end{array}\right)$

$\searrow$ P5

Where it moves down a perfect 5th

Remember where the bII7 comes from. $\left(\begin{array}{ccc} II & V & I \\ Dm & G7 & C \end{array}\right) - \left(\begin{array}{c} V7 \\ G7 \end{array}\right) - \left(\begin{array}{c} bII7 \\ Db7 \end{array}\right)$ are a tri-tone apart

The III7 chord (key of C) = Em7 can substitute for the I major 7 chord

Drop the root of the CM9 chord and you produce Em7.

C maj. 9 = C E G B D

The IIIm7 or III7
 Em7 or E7   will move to the VI degree Am7 or A7

The bIII7   Ebm7
            Eb7   will move down $\frac{1}{2}$ step to Dm7 or the bVI degree Abm7 or Ab7

Remember the rule about a minor 7th chord always substituting a dom. 7th chord - delaying the movement of V7 to I or the tri-tone Dom7 (G7 → Db7)

Ex. 1) (G7 C) use (Dm7 G7 C) (Dm7 Db7 C) (Dm7 Abm7 Db7 C)
     2) (A7 D7 G7 C) use (Em7 to A7) (Am7 to D7) (Dm7 to G7) etc. =
     2) Em7 A7, Am7 D7, Dm G7, C.

The IV chord functions mostly with II7 and I but because it is a major 7th quality, it can function as a tonal center in transition passages.

Key of C to $\underline{\text{gm7} \quad \text{C7} \quad \text{Fmaj.7}}$) $\underline{\text{Fm7}}$ Em7 Dm7 G7 C
$\qquad\qquad\quad$ Key of F

The VIm7 and VI7 chords move down a 5th to the II chord or $\frac{1}{2}$ step to the $\flat$VI chord; again employing the 2 strongest movements.

The I maj. 6 chord = C E G A. The VIm7 chord = A C E G.
Both have the same letters and VIm7 can substitute the I 6 chord.

Also we use the VI chord in a deceptive cadence;

$$\left(\begin{matrix} \text{Dm7} & \text{G7} & \text{C}\triangle\text{7} \\ \text{II} & \text{V7} & \text{I}\triangle\text{7} \end{matrix}\right) \quad \text{or} \quad \left(\begin{matrix} \text{Dm7} & \text{G7} & \text{Am7} \\ \text{II} & \text{V7} & \text{VI7} \end{matrix}\right) \quad \text{Am7 substitutes the C}\triangle\text{7 chord.}$$

$\qquad\qquad\qquad\qquad\qquad\qquad\qquad$ Dm7
Again, think of the substitution: Am7 to D7 to G7 to C$\triangle$7
$\qquad\qquad\qquad\qquad\qquad\quad$ VIm7 to II7 to V7 to I$\triangle$7

The $\flat$VI7 (tri-tone of II7) moves to V or to the $\flat$II. (A$\flat$7 to G7 or A$\flat$7 to D$\flat$7)
$\qquad\qquad\qquad\qquad\qquad\qquad$ ($\frac{1}{2}$ step) $\qquad\qquad$ (5th)

The VII∅ chord (B D F A) substitutes the V9 chord (G B D F A)
$\qquad$ Bm7$\flat$5 $\qquad\qquad\qquad\qquad\qquad\qquad\qquad\qquad$ G9

If you drop the root of the G9 chord, you will have the Bm7$\flat$5 chord.

The $\flat$VII7 is preceded by the IVm7 chord to form its own tonality.

$\qquad\qquad\quad$ Ex (Fm7 $\quad$ B$\flat$7 $\quad$ E$\flat\triangle$7)
$\qquad\quad$ Key of C IVm7 $\quad\flat$VII7 $\quad$ I maj7
$\qquad\qquad\qquad$ $\lfloor$ E$\flat$tonality $\qquad\qquad$ $\rfloor$

It can also move by 5th. $\quad\flat$VIIm7 $\qquad$ B$\flat$m7
$\qquad\qquad\qquad\qquad\qquad\flat$VII7 $\quad$ or $\quad$ B$\flat$7 $\quad$ to E$\flat$ or E$\flat$m or E$\flat$7

Vm7 moves to I7. $\quad$ (C $\quad$ Dm7 $\quad$ Gm7 $\quad$ C7 $\quad$ F$\triangle$7
$\qquad\qquad\qquad\qquad$ I $\quad$ IIm7 $\quad$ Vm7 $\quad$ I7 $\quad$ IV$\triangle$7
$\qquad\qquad\qquad\qquad$ $\lfloor$ $\nearrow$5th $\qquad\qquad$ $\rfloor$

$\qquad\qquad\qquad\qquad$ Key of F

If there is one vital function the bass must perform in a group, it is to know at all times what harmony is being played and what are the common substitutions used.

In the following drill in the key of F major, the student is to take each chord of the scale both diatonic (using scale notes) and non-diatonic (using notes not in the scale) and write a common progression using the movement of a 5th, $\frac{1}{2}$ step and substitution studied above.

Key of F Diationic and Non-Diatonic Chords

Ex - II7 = gm7 (II7 V7 I) then play this progression
gm7 c7 F△7

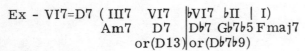

Ex - VI7=D7 (III7   VI7 |♭VI7 ♭II | I)
Am7   D7 |D♭7 G♭7♭5 Fmaj7
or(D13)|or(D♭7♭9)

The student must have at his fingertips all the chords in the often played keys and at least a working knowledge of the harmonies in these pregressions until they are familiar in the more remote keys. Practice singing and hearing.
At this stage of the book, the student should be able to hear intervals with accuracy and speed. This will help to recognize the substition chords in progressions.

Blues

Every jazz artist knows the blues progression. Most fine players use more than one set of changes in their approach to blues playing. The bass player should be prepared to substitute freely and play these more common approaches to blues stylings.

① The blues progression is a 12 bar progression that uses basically I IV V chords.

The 1st four bars use	I or I7 chord + substitutions of the I + IV7 chord
The 2nd four bars use	IV + IV7 harmonies or substitutions leading to the I or I7 chords
The 3rd four bars use the	V7 chord or (II7 V7) + substitutions of these chords leading back to I or I7

Another interpretation is

②
1st 4 Bars   I or I7

Next 2 Bars   IV7

Next 2 Bars   I or I7

Next 2 Bars   V7 + IV7

Next 2 Bars   I + V7

Blues in F ♯1 Interpretation

The most important concept here is that the student memorize the basic changes in a few keys (C, Bb, Eb) and writes or creates his own lines. Everything at this stage should be directed towards self-expression and development of individual style.

Blues in Bb ♯2 Interpretation

Now play your own chords and then play the changes in the keys of F, Eb, Ab, C, G.

Blues changes have become much more interesting and exciting in the evolving years. The basic harmonic structure is kept but the new harmonies and substitutions produce different melodic concepts.

The following progression which uses altered and substitution harmonies should be played in arpeggio and scale patterns before attempting to create jazz choruses.

Blues in B♭

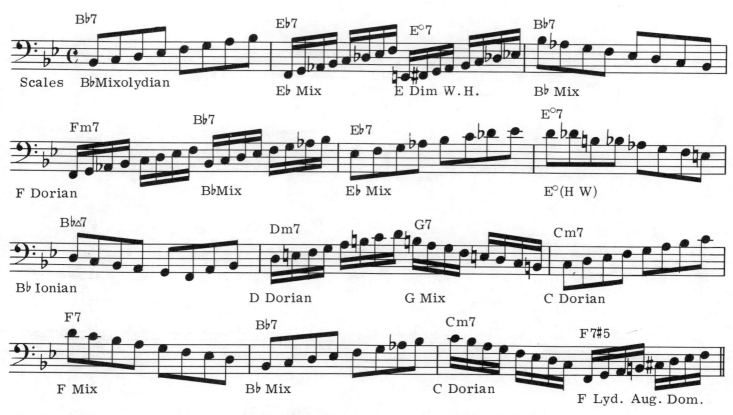

Scales   B♭ Mixolydian   E♭ Mix   E Dim W.H.   B♭ Mix

F Dorian   B♭ Mix   E♭ Mix   E°(H W)

B♭ Ionian   D Dorian   G Mix   C Dorian

F Mix   B♭ Mix   C Dorian   F Lyd. Aug. Dom.

Now play ideas over the above changes.

Blues #4 Interpretation

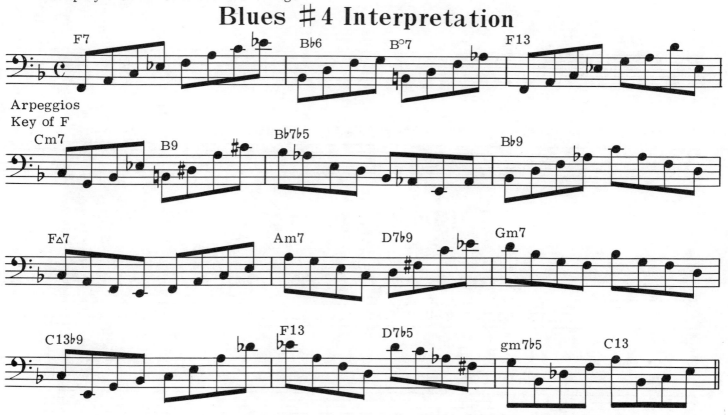

Arpeggios
Key of F

The student must play 2 complete different sets of arpeggios before attempting to play a jazz chorus. By playing the scales and arpeggios to these chords the student increases his vocabulary for jazz ideas.

Blues Pattern

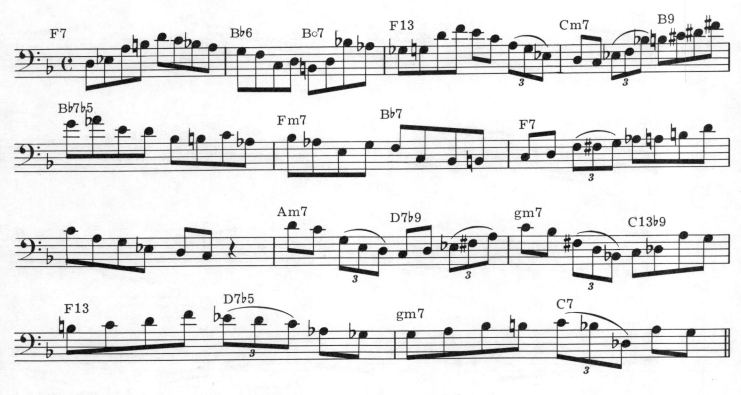

Blues Pattern #5

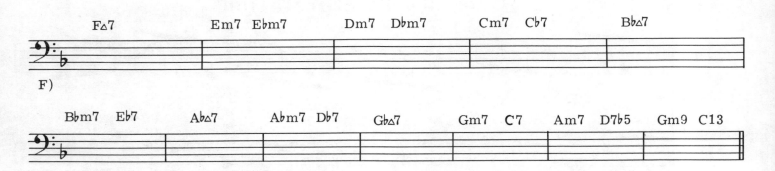

Blues Pattern #6

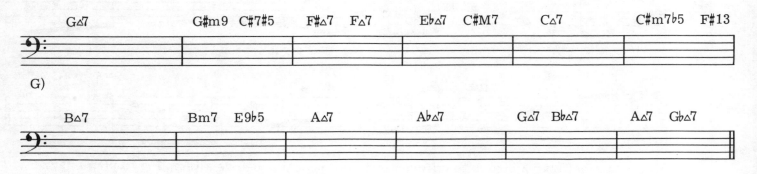

Invent your own – there are endless versions.

Musical terms

Dynamic signs
PP - Pianissimo - Very softly
P - Piano - Softly
FP - Forte piano - Loud, then immediately softer
MF - Mezzo forte - Medium loud
F - Forte - Loud
FF - Fortissimo - Very loud
SFZ - Sforzando - With sudden force

CRESC. ◁ CRESCENDO - Increase the volume

DECRESC. ▷ DECRESCENDO

DIM. ▷ DIMINUENDO   Decreasing the volume

Tempo markings
M.M. - Metronome marking - ♩ = 120 (120 Quarter notes per minute)
TEMPO - Rate of speed of a musical piece
GRAVE, ADAGIO, LENTO - Very slow tempos
ANDANTE, ANDANTINO, MODERATO - Slow to moderate tempos
ALLEGRETTO - Happy, a little faster than moderato
ALLEGRO, PRESTO, VIVACE - Very fast tempos
AD - LIB - Play freely, not in strict time
Rubato
ACCEL. - Accelerando - Increase the speed
(RIT. - Ritard   )   Gradual slowing of the speed
(RALL. - Rallendo)
TENUTO - Hold for full time

⌢ OR FERMATA - Hold or pause - Hold written character for longer value
A TEMPO - In the original tempo
Other signs
FINE - End   DA CAPO - From the beginning
D.C. AL FINE - From the beginning to the word fine

DAL SEGNO (D.S.) - From the sign 𝄋

D.S. AL FINE - From the sign to the word fine
CODA - Closing -
SEGUE- - Continue
TACET - Do not play
GLISS - (Glissando) - Slide on the strings
GRACE NOTES - Small notes added for ornamental effect
LEGATO - Smooth, connected
STACATTO - Detached
TUTTI - All together
SEMPRE - Always
METER - The time signature of a piece (4/4 - 3/4) etc.
8VA - Octave higher
8 BASSO - Octave lower

The student at this time should not feel that this is the end of studying. The greatest teacher is review and the student should go through the book again playing the scales and arpeggios faster with more sound and learn his theory to the point where he has all the information at his fingertips. There is a nucleus of bass players today who have a technique that compares favorably with the conventional soloists in a group. They are pushing the technical capacity of bass players at an accelerated rate. There are various combos whose bass players are playing a new kind of harmonic scheme, one that follows the material outlined in this book. It behooves the student to digest this material thoroughly before he strikes out in new directions. The foundation for the coming years is in these pages and the student should do all he can to build a solid background. Rhythmical exercises should be learned to the point of memorization. Because of the length of this book, the author has not been able to get into the ultra -modern material leading to the 12-tone music of the 20th century. Stylings, orchestral accompaniements are covered adequately in the Mel Bay Studio Stage Band Bass studies and were not dealt with in this book. The student should begin memorizing tunes as soon as possible. Every professional should know at least 80 to 100 tunes before attempting to play with experienced players. Every serious student should own the finest instrument possible - one that plays in tune and produces a good sound. Finally, the bassist should cultivate the desire to be one of the best if not the best trained players in the group. He should develop some ability to play piano and at least know how to voice chords and play conventional jazz progressions.

First and foremost, be a musician. - The playing will follow.